S0-BEH-948

Drew University Studies in Liturgy Series
General Editors: Kenneth E. Rowe and Robin A. Leaver

The Language of the Psalms in Worship

American Revisions of Watts' Psalter

Drew Studies in Liturgy, No. 4

Rochelle A. Stackhouse

The Scarecrow Press, Inc.
Lanham, Md., & London
1997

BS
1435
.S73
1997

Revision of author's dissertation, *American Revisions of Watts' Psalter: Liturgical Change in the Early Republic,* completed for a Ph.D. in Liturgical Studies, 1994, from Drew University.

SCARECROW PRESS, INC.

Published in the United States of America
by Scarecrow Press, Inc.
4720 Boston Way
Lanham, Maryland 20706

4 Pleydell Gardens, Folkestone
Kent CT20 2DN, England

Copyright © 1997 by Rochelle A. Stackhouse

All rights reserved. No part of this publication may be reproduced, stored in a retrieval system, or transmitted in any form or by any means, electronic, mechanical, photocopying, recording, or otherwise, without the prior permission of the publisher.

British Cataloguing-in-Publication Information Available

Library of Congress Cataloging-in-Publication Data

Stackhouse, Rochelle A., 1957—
    The language of the Psalms in worship : American revisions of Watts' Psalter / Rochelle A. Stackhouse.
        p.   cm.—(Drew studies in liturgy ; no. 4)
    Revision of author's doctoral dissertation, Drew University.
    Includes bibliographical references.
    ISBN 0-8108-3267-4 (cloth : alk. paper)
    1. Bible. O.T. Psalms—Liturgical use.   2. Liturgical language—English.   3. Watts, Isaac, 1674–1748. Psalms of David imitated in the language of the New Testament.   4. Congregational churches—New England—Liturgy—History—18th century.   5. Reformed Church—New England—Liturgy—History—18th century.   6. Congregational churches—United States—Liturgy—History—19th century.
7. Reformed Church—United States—Liturgy—History—19th century.
I. Title. II. Series.
BS1435.S73   1997
264'.2—dc21   96-45995
                                                                   CIP

ISBN 0-8108-3267-4 (cloth:alk.paper)

♾ ™ The paper used in this publication meets the minimum requirements of American National Standard for Information Sciences—Permanence of Paper for Printed Library Materials, ANSI Z39.48–1984. Manufactured in the United States of America.

To Peter Gavin Ferriby
whose patience and humor and wisdom I love
and
to Luke Kim Stackhouse Ferriby
who likes to sing and dance

"The church with Psalms must shout
no door can keep them out."
George Herbert

CONTENTS

Preface

Particularities of language enshrine the aspirations and ethos of a nation and a culture, even when that nation and culture are part of a larger language-group. The new American national identity and culture at the end of the eighteenth century and the beginning of the nineteenth century involved changes in the English language that reflected the different political, theological and aesthetic environment in these newly-constituted United States. In this timely and illuminating study Dr. Stackhouse demonstrates that sensitivity with regard to liturgical language is not an exclusively modern concern but one that accompanied the birth of the nation.

In much contemporary writing and debate on the issue of liturgical language, there is a strong tendency to assume that it is an exclusively modern problem. Many of the specifics regarding inclusive/ exclusive, feminine/masculine, archaic/contemporary language in worship are recent phenomena. But the concept of the necessity of revising liturgical language within a changing political, social and theological context is much older. Watts' *Psalms of David Imitated in the Language of the New Testament* (1719) reflected the new environment within which British Christians then worshiped, following the so-called Bloodless Revolution (1688) and the new political and religious conditions created by the Bill of Rights (1689), which established the Protestant Succession. Thereafter the British Monarchy spoke in the different accents of Dutch (William of Orange) and German (the Georges of Hanover). These new political realities were reflected in the language of Isaac Watts' psalms, which quickly became the primary form of congregational song sung by Congregationalists at worship in colonial New England. But with the changing political context following the Revolutionary War, when the dependent colony became an independent nation, the familiar texts of the Watts psalms conveyed a semiotic frame of reference that no longer reflected the realities within which the then contemporary American worshipers lived and worked. Watts' psalms were therefore revised, not simply to eliminate overt Britishisms, but modified to express the singularity of the experience of American Christianity in this new era of independence and nationhood. These revisions therefore do not only record linguistic and geographical shifts: more fundamentally they reflect changes in philosophy, theology and, above all, identity. They are the semiotic markers that witness to the emergence of a specific American liturgical language that was in the process of being created by such revisers as John Mycall, Joel Barlow and Timothy Dwight.

This is the substance of Dr. Stackhouse's perceptive book, a revised form of the doctoral dissertation written for the Liturgical Studies program, Drew University. It is an important study of a neglected area that, among other things, demonstrates that theological and liturgical formation frequently occurs more through what is sung than what is simply heard.

Robin A. Leaver
Westminster Choir College of
Rider University and Drew
University

Introduction

In the spring of 1992, I took Robin Leaver's course on hymnology as part of the doctoral program in liturgical studies at Drew University. One of my assignments for the course was to write an essay looking at the history of music in one of the parts of my denominational tradition, the Congregational root of the United Church of Christ.[1] In the process of researching that paper, I discovered a cryptic note in Louis Benson's mammoth volume *The English Hymn* referring to Timothy Dwight's work in revising Isaac Watts' *Psalms of David Imitated* to make it more acceptable to newly free American churches.

By 1992 when I happened on this note, American Presbyterians, Methodists, Lutherans, Episcopalians, Disciples of Christ, the United Church of Christ, and others had either published or were in the process of publishing new hymnals which revised the language of hymns to reflect changing sensibilities around issues of race, gender, theology, and shifts in American English usage. The new hymnals did not herald the *beginning* of the conversation about the language of the churches' liturgy, but rather came in the midst of many years of passionate discussion and debate. "Inclusive language," which came to mean using language that did not exclude women, people of color, or the handicapped, had been a hot topic in mainline American churches since the late 1970s.

On one side of the debate, supporters of language change in liturgy urged the churches to be in the forefront of helping people think in more just ways about human beings and with more variety about the divine. Traditional language in worship was seen as destructive and irrelevant. "The systematic and almost exclusive use of

---

1. This paper was later expanded into the article "Hymns of Love and Praise: A Brief History of Music in American Congregational Churches." *Prism* 8 (Spring 1993): 38–52.

male God-language . . . gives a distorted vision of God and supports male dominance in church and society."[2]

Liturgical revisers went beyond language concerning gender, race, or handicap, however. Debates occurred concerning war or battle imagery and its inappropriate nature for churches that proclaim peace, the use of archaic pronouns such as "thee" and "thou" for God, and the penchant of hymn-writers of the past to refer to those of non-Christian faiths as "pagan" or "heathen."

Those opposed to such changes in the language of worship cited concerns for continuing the traditions of those who had come before, for maintaining the integrity of the poets who had written the hymns, for not allowing the church to simply blow with whatever breeze came along in a push to be relevant, and of the need to adhere in liturgy to an "orthodox" theology.

I had been both a listener and a participant in discussions of the language of worship, and particularly the language of hymns, since my seminary days in the late 1970s. As a pastor of two small churches, I struggled with this issue on a very practical level: what do we sing on a Sunday morning and what impact does it have on the lives and faith of the people who sing? Until I saw that footnote in Benson, however, I had never heard any discussion concerning whether language in hymns and liturgy had ever been changed before for any reason other than translation. As I traveled the road down which that note pointed me, I discovered that the language of hymns had not only been changed before, but changed often, and for reasons ranging from the political to the theological to the purely aesthetic. I also learned that those changes in the past often came not from rebels on the fringes of the church but from orthodox leaders in its midst.

My findings unearthed a whole new set of questions about liturgy in general. What is the purpose of worship and the language of worship? Does that language transcend time or reflect very specific times? Should it do either or both of those things? Who shapes the language of liturgy and what influences those shapers? What place do the worshipers have in shaping the language in which they worship? What impact do politics, art, literature, geography, and the development of a language have on what we say and sing in worship? What impact do ecclesiastical politics and change have? What role does worship play in shaping theology? Is it true, as Aidan Kava-

---

2. Brian Wren, *What Language Shall I Borrow?* (New York: Crossroad, 1989), 4.

nagh writes, that liturgy is "first order" theology and that doctrine is "second order," and what determines, then, what is "orthodox?"[3]

As a way of addressing some of those questions, then, I began to explore methodologies for discussing liturgical change. Specifically, I focused on the period of liturgical change in the legally established Congregational churches of Massachusetts and Connecticut between the American Revolution and the first third of the nineteenth century.

I owe a debt of gratitude to numerous scholars and librarians who assisted me in this project. Drew University Library, and especially Interlibrary Loan Librarian Josie Cook and Head of Reference Jody Caldwell, rendered many essential services. Though officially "retired," Alice Copeland provided much assistance and access to the Creamer Collection of hymnals at Drew, a collection which, when catalogued fully, will be of incalculable help to researchers in the field of hymnology. Admittance to the primary sources and the deep riches of the Benson collection was given with grace by Princeton Seminary Archivist William Harris and his assistant Doug Denne, and my deep gratitude goes to all the staff of Speer Library at Princeton Theological Seminary for this service to an alumna. The Beinecke Rare Books Library at Yale University, Harold Worthley of the Congregational Library in Boston, and Steve Pinell of the Organ Historical Society collection at Westminster Choir College, also shared resources and advice.

At Drew, Dr. Heather Elkins, Dr. Horton Davies, and Dr. Kenneth Rowe helped with resources and editorial suggestions. My deepest thanks go to Dr. Robin A. Leaver of Drew and Westminster Choir College whose good advice, wit, and vast book collection helped make this journey a delight. Thanks also to UCC Norwell for providing time and Bob and Rena Zeller for providing the place to complete this project. Finally thanks and love go to my husband, editor, indexer, resident library and computer expert, and friend, Peter Gavin Ferriby.

Rochelle A. Stackhouse
Oak Bluffs, Massachusetts
November, 1996

---

3. Aidan Kavanagh, *On Liturgical Theology* (New York: Pueblo, 1984), 83–85. Kavanagh's book itself raises a host of questions related to, but broader than, the scope of this study. It deserves more attention from the Protestant churches.

Chapter One

A New World

Introduction

The theologian of language Amos Wilder writes that "There is no 'world' for us until we have named and languaged and storied whatever is."[1] One of the ways Christians "name and language and story" the world occurs in the enactment of liturgy: prayers, sermons, sacraments, art, architecture, silence, and songs. These elements both reflect and create the identity of a worshiping community. That liturgical material interacts with the other names, language, and stories encountered by the worshipers in their social and political lives, both influencing and being influenced by the milieu outside the formal liturgical setting. The liturgy also interacts with theological and political currents within the church itself. In those contacts, liturgical change often occurs, as the "world" of the community at worship changes and finds a need for a new language, a new telling of old stories. That change happens regularly throughout church history, for though liturgy by nature is conservative and tends to change slowly, worshiping communities participate in the larger social, theological, and political changes occuring in any specific time.

Liturgy responds to those transformations in a variety of ways, usually reflecting the reactions of those in power who shape it. For example, the tremendous theological, social, and political upheaval of sixteenth-century Europe found voice in liturgies, from the extreme changes wrought in the liturgies of the Radical Reformers to the conservative reforms of the Council of Trent. A number of scholars looking at the various liturgies born in the sixteenth

---

1. Amos Wilder, "Story and Story-World," *Interpretation*, 37 (1983): 361.

1

century have seen reflections of the identity shifts in worshiping communities in their response to their times.[2]

In the American churches, some of them born in reaction to upheaval in Europe in the seventeenth century, the content of public worship also has influenced–and been influenced by—the social, political, and theological waves of the last four centuries. Scholars have explored, for example, the connections among the Jacksonian Democracy, the tremendous move of people to the frontier, and the theologies of the Second Great Awakening in the nineteenth century, all reflected in some way in the liturgies of the Camp Meetings.[3]

Lex credendi, lex orandi, and the world surrounding both move in a stream, and it is with that movement that this book is concerned. As Robert Taft writes, the purpose of studying liturgical history "is not to recover the past (which is impossible), much less to imitate it (which would be fatuous), but to *understand liturgy* which, because it has a history, can only be understood in motion, just as the only way to understand a top is to spin it."[4]

This volume explores an area of liturgical change, a time of "motion," in the Congregational churches of New England in the late eighteenth century, a time of considerable social, political, and theological upheaval in what was becoming the United States of America. The study examines three major American revisions of the English Independent Isaac Watts' *Psalms of David Imitated* of 1719 by John Mycall, Joel Barlow, and Timothy Dwight. All three of these editions appeared during this tumultuous period in American history.

The story actually begins in England in 1719 when Isaac Watts completed his plan to re-shape the Psalmody of English Independent Churches by publishing *The Psalms of David Imitated*. As chapter two will explain, Watts' Psalter provided a dramatic shift from metrical Psalmody which strove for close translation of Biblical text (whether or not the text was singable), to texts that "imitated" the Biblical Psalms but brought both poetic style and subject matter up-to-date for singers in early eighteenth-century England.

2. See, for example, Hughes Oliphant Old, "Daily Prayer in the Reformed Church of Strasbourg, 1525–1530," *Worship* 52 (1978): 121–138, or Elsie McKee, *John Calvin on the Diaconate and Liturgical Almsgiving* (Travaux d'Humanisme, 197), (Geneva: Droz, 1984).

3. James White, *Protestant Worship Traditions in Transition* (Louisville: Westminster/John Knox, 1989). See especially chapter 10 and his extensive Bibliography.

4. Robert Taft, *Beyond East and West: Problems in Liturgical Understanding* (Washington D.C.: Pastoral Press, 1984), 154.

That included numerous direct references within his Psalm texts to Great Britain, and several indirect allusions as well. Watts made these changes consistent with his Puritan heritage, which gave great importance to worship reflecting the experience of the worshipers.

Watts' Psalter found a market in Colonial America just as the fervor for revolution was beginning. Before the end of the revolutionary war, a printer in Newburyport, Massachusetts, John Mycall, saw that Watts' British references would present problems in a newly independent America. He published a revised version of Watts, changing the words to reflect the new political situation: the Psalmist no longer sang as a citizen of Great Britain, but of the United States of America.

Mycall got the early jump on the rapidly expanding market for revisions of Watts' work. The General Association of Connecticut (the body that joined in covenant the Congregational Churches of the state) commissioned Joel Barlow, a poet and one-time clergyman, in 1785 to make the "official" Congregational revision. Another commission followed in 1801, assigned by the Association to Timothy Dwight, grandson of Jonathan Edwards and then-president of Yale. Both Barlow and Dwight paid attention not only to the Britishisms, but to other facets of Watts' poetry as well. They also added versions of the twelve Psalms Watts had neglected to "imitate" because he felt they were unfit for Christian worship. Barlow's and Dwight's changes and additions speak volumes about the social, theological, ecclesiological, and political worlds in which they and the people of New England Congregational churches dwelt well into the nineteenth century. Many of their texts continued to influence the church's song well into the second half of the nineteenth century, and well beyond the New England Congregational tradition.

Only Louis F. Benson, a remarkable scholar and historian from the early 1900s, has considered these American revisions of Watts. He compiled a list of the editions of the revisions (see appendix one), along with brief commentary, in two articles in 1903 and 1904.[5] This current study is the first attempt at an extended critical evaluation of the works in their own context.

Methodology

Lawrence Hoffman, in his landmark work *Beyond the Text*, explores the process of liturgical change in American Judaism's Reform,

---

5. Louis F. Benson, "The American Revisions of Watts's 'Psalms,' " *Journal of the Presbyterian Historical Society*, II (1903–04): 18–34 and 75–89.

Conservative, and Reconstructionist movements. He traces how the different forms of the liturgy developed, noting that the forms both reflect and create identity for American Jews as distinct from their largely European homelands. In developing his theories of the significance of liturgical change, Hoffman notes:

> Whatever worshipers presume to say to God, they are at the same time directing a message to themselves. The very act of worship takes on the function of identifying for the worshipper what it is that he or she stands for, what real life is like, what his or her aspirations are. The liturgical medium becomes the message.[6]

Hoffman indicates that a central function of the study of liturgy is to seek out the message behind the medium as enacted in a worshiping community at a specific point in history. How did that message shape the liturgy itself? How did that message reflect the changes in the society at large, or in a worshiping community in particular, at a specific time and place? How was that message intended by its shapers to create the "world" of the worshipers who received it?

To arrive at answers to these questions, Hoffman proposes that we consider three aspects of any given liturgy: text (or in his words, content), structure, and choreography (or the enactment of the liturgy).[7]

In looking at the text in exploring liturgical change, we place emphasis on individual words: what words are substituted for what other words, and what can we learn about how those substitutions change meaning? What were they intended to signal about the world to the worshipers saying or singing them? Beyond the individual words, though, attention to the structure of the liturgy can reveal other messages: were parts of a traditional liturgy deleted or new parts added; was the order changed; was new importance given to once less significant parts of the liturgy; were parts renamed or redefined?

Finally, attention to changes in what Hoffman calls choreography, or how the worshiping community physically enacted the liturgy, can reveal insights into the broader changes. Does leadership shift; is there more or less participation by specific groups or individuals; does the physical location change; are books present where they once were not?

This final piece of Hoffman's methodology has its limitations,

---

6. Lawrence Hoffman, *Beyond the Text* (Washington, D.C.: Pastoral Press, 1984), 69.

7. Ibid., 70–71.

however, when dealing with history beyond living memory. Documentation of changes in choreography in worship for eighteenth- and nineteenth-century America is sketchy at best. What fleshes out that story, and completes the methodology for this study, is the insight from ritual studies that "to understand the meaning of ritual . . . is a movement of turning toward the social world of the ritual actors."[8] Understanding the context in which the liturgical changes were made contributes to our comprehension of the motivation behind the changes.

The liturgical scholar thus traces the importance and impact of any specific liturgical change on the identity of a worshiping community by examining text, structure, and choreography, informed by the insights of the social, political, and theological history of a time and place. This reveals, in Wilder's terms, the "world" of the worshiping community.

That will be the methodological center of this study. We will examine the specific liturgical changes (the content or text) by studying the exact word changes in the American revisions. We will explore the structure of the worship in which these Psalters were used through examination of contemporary books and articles as well as modern research materials. Records from the eighteenth and nineteenth centuries as well as more modern secondary sources will illuminate changes in choreography: how the Psalms were used in worship. The context of the time—sociological, political, and theological—will be studied in order to evaluate the influence of changing liturgy on the worshipers of Congregational churches, and what that may reveal about the life and struggles of the New England established churches on the eve of disestablishment.

To begin, this study will review the history, especially the liturgical, political, and theological history, of the New England churches up to and including the time of the American revolution. We will address the structure of worship as it evolved in the eighteenth century. Next, we will consider the history of English Psalmody and of Isaac Watts in particular. Having thus set the American revisions in context, the genesis of the three revisions will be explored as a prelude to analyzing specific changes in them, which we will then look at to discern how they both reflected and molded changes in politics, theology, and the emerging language and aesthetic of the United States. We will conclude with a discussion of the use of the texts in public worship, the important place they held in those times of change, and the implications the method behind them continues to have for liturgy today, a time when many churches once again are examining and changing the language of the church's song.

---

8. Nancy Jay, *Throughout Your Generations Forever* (Chicago: University of Chicago Press, 1992), 13.

Chapter Two

Church and State Walk Hand in Hand

Church and Society before the Revolution

In Eighteenth century America—in city, village, and countryside—the idiom of religion penetrated all discourse, underlay all thought, marked all observances, gave meaning to every public and private crisis."[1]

To modern generations, nurtured in public schools on the separation of church and state, Patricia Bonomi's assertion about colonial America seems exaggerated. Yet numerous scholars and the remaining written evidence of the time confirm her view. Bruce Kuklick enlarges upon her statement: "The church stood between the demands of the faith and the realities of the world."[2] In the case of the legally and historically established Congregational churches, the struggle as colonies became nation would be to keep not only the religious idiom, but their own particular expression of it, at the center of political, social, and family life. Much of the story of these American churches in the pre-revolutionary eighteenth century revolves around that struggle.

This endeavor only makes sense in light of the dramatic changes occurring in all aspects of American life as the century progressed. The upheaval in political, social, and theological spheres proved

---

1. Patricia Bonomi, *Under the Cope of Heaven* (New York: Oxford University Press, 1986), 3.
2. Bruce Kuklick, *Churchmen and Philosophers* (New Haven: Yale University Press, 1985), 9.

staggering, especially to the New England Congregational[3] churches, well-established with a hundred years or more of history in America behind them. In considering the impact of Watts in America and America's impact on the revisions of Watts, it is helpful to examine some of that upheaval.

Social Structure

Walter Nugent has determined that in 1700, the total colonial population of America was 250,000.[4] The population in any one region proved fairly homogenous at this date. Just 50 years later, the total colonial population had risen to 1,250,000, a factor of the birth rate in the colonies as well as an exploding birth rate in Europe, and by the revolution, 2.5 million people lived together in the 13 colonies. This rapid, exponential increase in population strained "the old ways past breaking point. New Englanders either stayed in their sheltered towns, 'old, stable, concentrated . . . clannish,' or they looked at long last to frontier, rural opportunities."[5]

Obviously the churches had to deal with this growth, not only in numbers, but in the variety of class and ethnicity. The law at the time in Massachusetts and Connecticut required each citizen to pay the equivalent of taxes to support *the* town church. Everyone was expected, again by law, to appear at that church for worship and instruction. One of the effects of pre-revolutionary growth was the appearance of "Second" and "Third" churches. This, along with divisions coming out of the Great Awakening (see page 13), contributed to the fragmentation of churches and eventually necessitated the formation of Associations to monitor clergy and church life (such as the General Association of Connecticut, which played an important part in post-revolutionary Congregational church life). These "consociations" began with the agreement known as the Saybrook Platform in 1708–09.

---

3. Throughout this book, I refer to the New England Congregational churches, a group that includes some of those who would later officially be identified as Presbyterian and engage in the "Plan of Union" in 1801. The Plan provided that the two bodies would not compete with each other in evangelizing the frontier of America (which at the time included Vermont and New York). The net result was a division of territory that left the Congregational Churches dominant in New England. Although the Presbyterians also used both Barlow's and Dwight's Watts, this volume concentrates on churches mostly in Massachusetts and Connecticut, which remain, to this day, Congregational in polity and heritage.

4. Walter Nugent, *Structures of American Social History* (Bloomington: Indiana University Press, 1981), 41.

5. Ibid., 46–47.

Perhaps a more profound effect of the new diverse population was felt ecclesiologically and theologically. Many of the new immigrants came from faith communities other than those of Puritan/Congregational/Presbyterian stock, and they clamored for the right to pay their "church tax" to support their own churches and not the established churches. "As a result, in 1727, Episcopalians in Massachusetts were allowed to pay their assessment to a clergyman of their faith, instead of to the Congregational pastor, in towns where there was an Episcopal minister."[6] Similar laws were passed in Connecticut providing for Quakers, Baptists, and Anglicans.

This, of course, was just the beginning, the first step toward the demands for complete separation of church and state that arose after the revolutionary war.

Politics

Horton Davies observes that

> In addition to its theological significance, the meetinghouse [i.e., the church building] functioned as a political center where town meetings were held by the community, and—in the earliest days—also as a military bastion where gunpowder was stored . . . . So it was a meetinghouse in both sacred and secular senses.[7]

As is still obvious in many New England towns today, the church building's location at the center of town, often "on the green," as well as the fact that it frequently was the largest public building (or the *only* public building) in town, made it an obvious choice for meetings, elections, debates, rallies, and other gatherings. So in terms of physical space, the life of the church and the life of the politics of the day continually intersected.

Beyond buildings and taxes, however, the threads of spiritual and secular thought in New England wove together in a complicated tapestry. Patricia Bonomi observes that throughout the eighteenth century a large proportion of local officials not only attended church on Sunday (thereby obeying the law) but were communing church members.[8] "Merchants and lawyers joined public officials as

---

6. Williston Walker, *A History of the Congregational Churches in the United States* (New York: Christian Literature Co., 1894), 234.

7. Horton Davies, *The Worship of the American Puritans 1629–1730* (New York: Peter Lang, 1990), 233.

8. The Halfway Covenant of 1662 had provided that children of "unregenerate" Christians (i.e., those who had not professed an experience of conversion before pastor and assembly) could be baptized despite the state

elders, deacons . . . in all northern colonies. That the church afforded
not only religious but political and social opportunities . . . can
hardly be doubted."[9] On an informal level, Bonomi indicates, worship gatherings and other church events provided an opportunity
for those in power to meet with each other and with the people of
the town, as well as possibly to influence or be influenced by the
preaching, praying, scripture reading, and Psalm singing of a service.
Preachers proved open and bold in speaking about and *to* the political leaders in their midst. Jonathan Edwards, in "Some Thoughts
Concerning the Present Revival of Religion in New England," used
a hermeneutic of contextualizing Scripture which Watts had used in
his Psalter.[10] Deriding "civil authority" for not doing more to promote the Great Awakening in Massachusetts, he quotes Psalm 2, "Be
wise now, ye rulers; be instructed, ye judges of New England: kiss
the Son, lest he be angry and ye perish from the way."[11] This cross-
fertilization was also publicly expressed in the regular "Election
Sermons" given throughout the colonial period and the early republic, which all the political officials of a town would attend.[12]

Up to the revolution, the religious and the political life of town
and colony heavily influenced each other. Any textbook of American history describes in detail the political upheavals of the century,
which naturally impacted clergy and lay members of the churches.
Territorial expansion, the French and Indian War, the growing dis-

---

of their parents. This opened the door to a two-tier church membership:
those who communed and had "proven" their conversion and those who
attended but did not commune. See Walker, 170ff. This practice gave rise
to the discrepancies in later authors who attempted to determine actual
membership figures for colonial churches. To catalog only *communing*
members as some authors (such as Roger Finke, *The Churching of America
1776–1990* [Rutgers University Press, 1992]) seem to do gives a distorted
picture of actual church participation.

9. Bonomi, *Cope*, 102.

10. See *Psalmody* below. Watts, through the use of subtitles as well as
paraphrases of the Psalm texts, applied specific Psalms to historical events,
as in Psalm 115, "A Psalm for the 5th of November."

11. Jonathan Edwards "Some Thoughts Concerning the Present Revival
of Religion in New England," *The Works of Jonathan Edwards*, Vol. 4 (New
Haven: Yale University Press, 1985), 373.

12. Examples abound of these sermons, many noted in Sprague, *Annals
of the American Pulpit*, 1857. Ebenezer Pemberton preached the "Artillery
Election Sermon"in 1756 at New Brick Church in Boston, Jonathan Todd
preached a "Connecticut Election Sermon" in East Guilford,Connecticut
in 1749, etc; see also Alice Baldwin, *The New England Clergy and the
American Revolution* (Durham: Duke University Press, 1928), 5 and
passim.

content with English policies toward the colonies (the Molasses Act of 1733, the Sugar Act of 1764, Stamp Act of 1765, the Boston Massacre of 1770, and especially the perceived threat of an Anglican Bishop coming to America in the 1760s), and the emerging factionalism of colonial politicians into what would become Loyalists and Patriots all proved pivotal issues. New England church members and clergy found themselves beset by dramatic change or threat of change on all fronts, and reacted to that change in the context of a religion-centered life. Obviously, the internal affairs of the churches could not remain unaffected by the growing turmoil around them.[13]

Theology and Church Politics

Throughout this period, as has often been the case in the history of the church, developments in theology and church politics followed convergent courses. The Puritans who arrived from England in the previous century came with a clear theological and ecclesiological vision: worship should be free of set forms and relevant to the day and people. "This means that relevance really has a priority almost equal to biblical authority, so that relevance and authenticity are united."[14] In addition, worshipers should be free to form their own local church, call their own pastor, and govern their own affairs. The Puritans supported an ecclesiology based on local autonomy, but with limitations. That autonomy had to fit into the Puritan understanding of "church" and uphold the same doctrine and essentially the same practices as other Puritans.

Their outlook was millennial, feeling that Boston was a "city set on a hill to show the world what truly reformed religion, especially worship, was like."[15] These colonists embodied the "faithful remnant" of the covenant who would forge, with God, a new Zion. Along with millennialism, they believed strongly in predestination, and they were clear on *their* destination as eternal salvation. In addition, they perceived of God as specially present, immanent, in this chosen land.

> Correlative to predestination was the strong belief in special providence. This was the conviction of Puritans that in the events of national, ecclesiastical, familial and individual life, one must search for

---

13. For more on church/state relations in the years leading to the American revolution see the bibliography for works by Mark Noll, Nathan Hatch, and Sidney Mead.

14. James White, *Protestant Worship: Traditions in Transition* (Louisville: Westminster/John Knox, 1989), 119.

15. Ibid., 127.

the hidden hand of God . . . . Hence life itself became a second scripture through which the Written Word might be better understood.[16]

Puritan theology stood on Calvinism, filtered by the subsequent
Reformed tradition in Switzerland, the Netherlands, Scotland, and
England. Their music was the Psalms; their reading was the scrip-
tures.

Bruce Kuklick sums up the Puritans of the seventeenth century
by noting "they brought not only a strong theological orientation,
but also tenacious communal impulses, utopian aspirations, a sense
of being chosen, and a belief in social and religious exclusivity and
uniformity."[17]

As the colonial population grew and diversified, Puritan theology
and ecclesiology faced dissent and underwent modification. The descendants of the Puritans, the Congregationalists and Presbyterians
of the eighteenth century, witnessed battles between Calvinists and
those accused of Arminianism (including Methodists), the rum-
blings that became American Unitarianism and Universalism, and
the division of clergy into Old and New Light and later Old and
New Divinity. This division resulted in some places in "separatist"
churches, many of which later became Baptist.

The largest upheaval theologically and ecclesiologically before the
revolution was what has come to be called the First Great Awakening.[18] While such religious leaders as Jonathan Edwards initially wel-
comed this seemingly spontaneous rise in religious enthusiasm
among New England church members, others believed otherwise.
Ezra Stiles, President of Yale, summed up this perspective by saying
in 1761 that "Multitudes were seriously, soberly and solemnly out
of their wits."[19]

No agreement exists on exactly what prompted this emotional,
conversion/repentance/forgiveness-based revival among the descendants of the Puritans, but without question, the preaching of the
English evangelist George Whitefield had a major impact in spread-
ing it. Whitefield, an Anglican/Methodist, used an emotion-wrench-
ing style of preaching that spared no one—including clergy—from

---

16. Davies, *Worship*, 26.
17. Kuklick, *Churchmen*, 9.
18. For more complete treatments of the First Great Awakening, including scholarly conflict surrounding it as well as the Second Great Awakening
as the century turned, see Bonomi, *Under the Cope of Heaven*; Kuklick,
Churchmen and Philosophers; Alan Heimert and Perry Miller, *The Great
Awakening: Documents Illustrating the Crisis and Its Consequences*, New
York, 1967.
19. Cited in Nugent, *Structures*, 46.

the need for public, expressive action to show that they truly believed in God and repented of their sins. Whitefield and his disciples named clergy members suspected of being unregenerate and even encouraged their congregations to get rid of them. Obviously this promoted division in the ranks, which became codified as "New Light" or revival supporters versus the "Old Light" strict Calvinists who opposed the revival tactics and who wielded considerable political power in the church.[20] In 1745 in Connecticut, in fact, the Old Light majority in the General Association of the Colony of Connecticut took the following action:

> Whereas there has of late years been many Errors in Doctrine and Disorders in Practice, prevailing in the Churches of this Land, which seem to have a threatening aspect upon these Churches; and whereas Mr. George Whitefield has been the Promoter, or at least the Faulty occasion of many of these Errors and Disorders, this Association think it needfull for them to declare that if the said Mr. Whitefield should make his progress thro' this Government, it would by no means be advisable for any of our Ministers to admitt him into their Pulpits, or for any of our people to attend upon his Preaching and Administrations.
>   Voted in the Affirmative.[21]

Yet Whitefield's influence did not bypass Connecticut churches.

Stephen Berk describes the ecclesiological results of the Great Awakening for the churches as follows: "the Great Awakening split Puritanism into four antagonistic factions. On Connecticut's Evangelical side were New Light Congregationalists who sought to control the Standing Order." Baptists and Separatists who rejected ecclesiasticalism formed the second group. The third were Old Calvinists or Old Light, "heirs of traditional New England Puritanism" believing in "a God who prescribes rational requirements for religion." The fourth group was Arminians, accused of making Calvinism into works righteousness.[22] This division of the clergy would continue throughout the revolutionary period and be renamed as new conflicts over theology and church government arose.

---

20. Bonomi, *Cope*, 150 and 152.

21. *The Records of the General Association of the Colony of Connecticut, June 20, 1738–June 19, 1799* (Hartford: Case, Lockwood and Brainard, 1888), 17.

22. Stephen Berk, *Calvinism versus Democracy: Timothy Dwight and the Origins of American Evangelical Orthodoxy* (Hamden, Conn: Archon Books, 1974), 10–11.

Worship

Beyond church politics, the Great Awakening impacted theology and worship in some dramatic and lasting ways. The millennial stress of the Puritans was strengthened by the Awakening,[23] as well as the tendency to see God in earthly matters. Natural idioms in preaching became paradigms for human relations with God (as in the spider in Edwards' famous sermon "Sinners in the Hands of an Angry God"). The call for individual "conversion experiences" fostered "the new Spirit of defiant individualism that was one of the most radical manifestations of the Awakening."[24]

Worshipers, no longer content to sing the long, tedious metrical Psalms brought over on the Mayflower or subsequent ships, began to sing the hymns and Psalms of Isaac Watts. Not only the words of singing, but the style and the music changed. "Regular singing," i.e., in unison or harmony stanza by stanza, as opposed to lining out and responding to a precentor or cantor as had been the custom, became the norm. Composers such as William Billings wrote new, more engaging tunes and opened "Singing Schools" to teach the new tunes and styles.[25] This development sparked division among the churches, with the Old Light party generally opposing the innovations in Psalmody wrought by Watts and the new tunesmiths, while others, such as Edwards and the New Light party, supported Watts' hymns and Psalm "imitations."[26] The Old Light party still believed that strict fidelity to the biblical Psalms was necessary in worship. At the eve of the revolution, public Sunday worship, with the exception of the style and content of singing and preaching in some places, was still conducted much along the lines of the early Puritan simplicity seen in worship in the Colonies from the early seventeenth century. Horton Davies, relying on reports from John Cotton, describes the typical service form, repeated twice each Sunday:

Opening Prayer of Intercession and Thanksgiving
Reading and exposition of a chapter of the Bible

---

23. Henry F. May, *The Enlightenment in America* (New York: Oxford University Press, 1976), 54.

24. Bonomi, *Cope*, 158.

25. Louis F. Benson, *The English Hymn* (Richmond: John Knox, 1915), 169ff.

26. Edwards' congregation in Northampton began to sing Watts in 1742 at least once a Sunday, though not without some controversy. See Edwards' letters in *Proceedings of the Massachusetts Historical Society*, X (Boston: The Society), 429.

Psalm Singing
Sermon
Psalm Singing
Prayer
Blessing [27]

Though the style of each of the components might change, and sacraments be added as needed (i.e., monthly or bi-monthly Lord's Supper, baptisms, and collection in the afternoon), this form of service probably continued into the nineteenth century. Of course, the revivals of both Great Awakenings would have differed from this format,[28] but the typical eighteenth-century New England Congregational Church would have met for worship in this liturgical style each Sunday. Church histories of the period rarely mention anything at all about the worship services themselves except prayer, Psalm, and preaching.[29]

As the revolutionary period progressed, this simple liturgical form remained standard for New England Congregationalism, one of the few things about life in New England that remained static before the turn of the century. A consideration of the impact of the revolution and the years of the early republic on church life—and the influence of churches on the republic—will show the immediate context for the Mycall, Barlow, and Dwight revisions of the Watts Psalter.

Church and Society from the Revolution to 1800

Standard accounts of the American revolution tend to overlook or downplay the role of the clergy and churches in bringing America to revolt and through it to nationhood. The great folk heroes of the time, people such as Thomas Jefferson, John Adams, and Benjamin Franklin, are often depicted as having little to do with organized religion.

Church historians, however, have made varying claims for the considerable influence of clergy and worship on the course of the revolution. The central thesis of Alice Baldwin's classic work on the

---

27. Davies, *Worship*, 16.

28. See Adams, *Meeting House to Camp Meeting*, for more detail on revivals.

29. Indeed, the great bulk of the church histories surveyed for this book allot much more space to building and organizational matters, as well as descriptions of disputes with the clergy, than with anything concerning worship. See chapter 6 and bibliography.

role of the New England clergy in the revolution asserts that many important Massachusetts and Connecticut ministers literally laid the theological and philosophical groundwork for liberty many years before the beginning of the war in 1775. Baldwin believes that the Continental Congress recognized this fact by calling several Fast and Thanksgiving Days in 1774. This gave the clergy opportunities to preach political sermons which would be published subsequently as patriotic pamphlets.[30] Nathan Hatch links Great Awakening theology and practice directly with the formation of a new democratic nation after the war was over, when ". . . many humble Christians in America began to redeem a dual legacy. They yoked strenuous demands for revivals, in the name of George Whitefield, with calls for the expansion of popular sovereignty, in the name of the revolution."[31] Certainly organized religion and its leaders, including Congregational New England clergy and lay people, found themselves responding in a variety of ways to the new upheavals of the periods of the revolutionary war and the early republic to follow. Once again, those upheavals helped set the stage for changes in the words and acts of worship.

Social Structure

Usually during a war population growth of an affected nation slows, and the colonies during the revolution followed that pattern. Birth rates were lower, immigration decreased, many Loyalists moved to Canada or Europe—including disproportionate numbers of the upper classes of the colonies and many Anglicans.

Following the war, the population began to change dramatically, not only in numbers but in social structure. The change accelerated as the nation entered a period of population growth unmatched in any period since, including the post-World War II baby boom.[32] This resulted in a third of the entire population of the United States in 1800 being under the age of ten.[33]

Much of that younger population, however, did not stay in New England. They were the younger sons and daughters of farmers who would not inherit much land of their own, and so went to the fron-

---

30. Baldwin, *New England Clergy*, 123; see also Peter Carroll, ed. *Religion and the Coming of the Revolution* (Waltham, Massachusetts: Ginn Blaisdell, 1970), for examples.

31. Nathan Hatch, *The Democratization of American Christianity* (New Haven: Yale University Press, 1989), 6–7.

32. Nugent, *Structures*, 52.

33. Ibid., 56.

tier (New York, Vermont, later Ohio) after the war to settle. This impacted New England Congregationalists in two major ways: it meant smaller population growth in the already established churches (Nugent notes that fertility rates in those who migrated was considerably higher than in those who stayed),[34] and it spurred them to move into mission and church planting in the new territories. Of course, this mission work also was taken on by the Baptists, Methodists, and other, newer church bodies. Nugent observes that this migration of young adults contributed to stability in settled New England by removing those most likely to agitate and cause trouble through restlessness.[35] So while population changes on one hand moved the established churches into mission opportunities, it also left the majority of the generation in power in pre-revolutionary New England *in* New England while much of the next generation migrated north and west. The entrenchment of the powerful in church (and state to a somewhat lesser extent, especially in Connecticut[36]), undoubtedly affected the spiritual lives of the remaining populace. Richard Hathaway observes that, in the last part of the eighteenth century,

> Yankee minds, like many others, were full of such contradictions . . . .
> Loyalty to the past, the conservative principle, conflicted with the lure
> of the future, the principle of change, adventure, romantic excite-
> ment.[37]

This split—between loyalty to the past and the urge to move into a dynamic new future—helped characterize social, political, and religious conflicts arising in the last quarter of the century. In the middle of those two poles stood a place of anxiety and uncertainty filled by a variety of religious, philosophical, and political responses to the age. That anxious middle space, Nathan Hatch believes, can be defined by three "realities about life in the early republic . . ."

---

34. Ibid., 68.

35. Ibid., 86.

36. Charles Keller notes that Connecticut during the revolution was one of the most completely self-governing colonies. "The Revolution caused less change in the ruling class, less political and social upheaval, than was the case in the erstwhile British colonies." *The Second Great Awakening in Connecticut* (New Haven: Yale University Press, 1942), 4. I believe that the reality was not quite as Keller saw it, however, as social and national political changes impacted Connecticut as other New England states.

37. Richard Hathaway, *Sylvester Judd's New England* (University Park: Penn State University Press, 1981), 60.

1. fear that the union might not work;
2. the new mobility which cut people off from family, church, roots, community;
3. the "splintering" of American Protestantism.[38]

Hatch goes so far as to say that the "real" American revolution encompassed far more than the split with England and its King.

> The rejection of an ancient regime and the struggle to establish a new social and political order involved intense social strain and dislocation toward the end of the 18th century . . . . This vast transformation, this shift away from the Enlightenment and classical republicanism toward vulgar democracy and materialistic individualism in a matter of decades, was the real American revolution.[39]

To use Wilder's idiom, the American people were "languaging" and "storying" a whole new world in more than just the political realm, and the churches needed to respond to it and to the anxieties arising out of its formation.

The people who sought to shape not just a new nation but also a new culture were also some of the most literate people in the Western world, and that capacity and hunger for reading influenced both the political and religious lives of the new Americans. David Hall observes:

> Religion in New England embodied a distinctive mode of literacy, a mode originating in the Reformation . . . . The godly . . . valued direct access to the Word of God as the most precious of their privileges. Thus did literacy figure at the heart of cultural politics; thus did it represent the freedom that these people proclaimed for themselves.[40]

New Englanders for the most part could read published sermons and broadsides in addition to the Bibles and primers that taught them to read. A literate population could think for itself and evaluate ideas, and therefore, a mighty printing industry arose to shape those ideas, both political and religious. Watts' Psalter, and its revised versions, played a major role in that industry. The Psalter, the Bible, the primer, and the catechism were key texts in teaching literacy skills to children and adults alike. Joseph Buckingham, a servant in Connecticut, remembered spending Saturday evenings reciting the Westminster Catechism and

---

38. Hatch, *Democratization*, 63.

39. Ibid., 23.

40. David Hall, *Worlds of Wonder, Days of Judgement* (New York: Alfred Knopf, 1989), 18.

such Psalms or Hymns as I might have committed to memory in the course of the week. There was a time when I could recite Watts's version of the Psalms from beginning to end, together with many of his Hymns and Lyric poems.[41]

Clearly religious books shaped the cultural, and probably political, lives of New Englanders as much as their spiritual lives.

Politics

Obviously, the major political tumult involved replacing the rule of the King in England with a democratic form of government that united thirteen very diverse colonies into a single national government. This took place at a time when European political philosophy underwent considerable change under the influence of Locke, Rousseau, and other philosophers who questioned many Christian beliefs. This Enlightenment philosophy translated to the American leaders in a variety of ways. Henry May summarizes the "middle ground" taken by American political philosophy, including that of a number of New England Calvinists, as understanding that liberty "was associated above all with rationality."[42] That rationality fed political sermons and tracts during the War, as the logic of personal liberty against an oppressor seemed inescapable.

After the war, however, that rationalism traveled in a variety of political and religious directions. As the new republic formed, New England politics galvanized into two opposing parties: Thomas Jefferson's followers who favored disestablishment of religion (among many other things) and the Federalists (including the vast majority of leading New England Congregational clergy) who virulently opposed disestablishment.

According to clergy in Connecticut, a Federalist stronghold which did not officially disestablish the church until 1818, disestablishment and those who supported it were seeking to promote a rationalistic atheism that would undermine moral and social order. The primary example of such a result stood before the eyes of all Americans, these clergy felt, in the French revolution.

In many ways, the revolution in France affected the churches in the United States as much or more than the American revolution did.

The European political situation lent itself to the interpretation that an Infidel International was deliberately fostering the overthrow of all

---

41. Ibid., 37.
42. May, *Enlightenment*, 94.

religion and all government—that it had been successful in France and was pushing out from there. It was in New England that the controversy became hottest . . . . There the Congregational churches were established, and their clergy—Federalist almost to a man—were inclined to identify True Religion with the Standing Order.[43]

Despite the fact that New England Congregationalists tended to be rabidly anti-Roman Catholic, they viewed the fate of the established Church in France with alarm. As reports of violence and complete social disintegration reached the United States, the clergy became vociferous in their concern that the same thing not happen in their States. For many years the leading clergy had been speaking out about the moral degeneration that inevitably accompanied war.[44] Now they witnessed that degeneration taken to an extreme and yoked with Deism, Rationalism, and an atheism that raised the Goddess of Reason in the place of the God of Abraham and Sarah. Undoubtedly, the clergy also worried about the collapse of the social strata that separated the classes of pre-revolutionary France. "Calvinistic New Englanders, with their abiding fear of uncontained desire, were horrified at the French abandonment of their traditional order."[45]

The Congregational clergy found reason to believe that the influence of the French chaos had permeated some of the philosophical and political leadership of their new nation as well. Jefferson personified this potential for disaster, but others preceded him in their writings, including some heroes of the American revolution, at least one of whom had been a Congregational clergyman from Connecticut:

> by the end of the century the French Revolution provided a compelling example of extreme republicanism accompanied by "practical atheism." In the United States, Ethan Allen, Joel Barlow, and Tom Paine were leading figures of a nascent movement of free-thinkers.[46]

Indeed, in a Fast Day sermon in May of 1798, The Rev. Jedidiah Morse of Charlestown, Massachusetts, saw as "the main source of

---

43. Sidney Mead, *The Lively Experiment: The Shaping of Christianity in America* (New York: Harper and Row, 1963), 50–51.

44. Timothy Dwight is quoted as having said that "War is at least as fatal to morals as to life, or happiness" in reference to the American revolution. Cited in Adolf Koch, *Religion and the American Enlightenment* (New York: Thomas Crowell, 1933), 246.

45. Berk, *Calvinism*, 39.

46. Kuklick, *Churchmen*, 48.

American dangers" our relations with France and those influenced by its philosophy and action, such as Allen, Barlow, Paine and others.[47]

Theology and Church Politics

American politics on state and national levels contained varying levels of chaos and controversy between the revolution and the turn of the century. Theological and political upheaval in the church clearly rivaled secular politics in its impact on the spiritual lives of New England Congregationalists. Patricia Bonomi records that

> when one farmer who had fought at Concord Bridge was asked years later whether he was defending the ideas of such liberal writers, he declared that for his part he had never heard of Locke or Sidney, his reading having been limited to the Bible, the Catechism, Watts's Psalms and Hymns and the Almanac.[48]

The farmer might have added that he also probably heard few speeches on Locke or Sidney, but plenty of sermons and prayers that used, or abused, their work, and that later strongly criticized the writings and speeches of political philosophers, theologians, politicians, and church leaders. The last quarter of the eighteenth century in the churches was not a time of neutrality, and all aspects of church life reflected this discord.

Some of the religious upheavals of the period continued currents that had flowed through American Congregationalism for over a century. One such theological theme is the prevalence of millennialism in Congregational (indeed all Calvinist groups') theology. Clearly, the millennial significance of the American revolution shone through to church leaders. During the War, the Rev. Wheeler Case published a poem to "aid the glorious cause of Liberty" which included the following lines:

> Our borders shall extend both far and wide,
> Our cords shall lengthen out on every side,
> State after State, the growing numbers rise,
> The greatest Empire this below the skies
>
> . . . .
> Here every sort of fruit springs up and grows,
> And all the *Land with milk and honey flows*.[49]

---

47. Koch, *Religion and the American*, 251.
48. Bonomi, *Cope*, 5.
49. Baldwin, *New England Clergy*, 166. Italics in original.

This identification of America with the New Israel appears from the earliest Puritan documents, and would continue to appear throughout the revolution as the purity of America was contrasted to the vice of England, and the victory of the United States seen as God's judgement on England.[50]

Some writers consider that this millennial vision declined in established churches after the revolution and was transferred, perhaps, to the deists on one hand and the newer, revivalist churches on the other. Bonomi writes, for example, that as the new republic began, religion did not decline, "but something else, something perhaps loftier: a veritable utopia—or rather a utopian vision, one that had shone brightest at the very moment of the Puritan exodus from Old England to New" began to decay.[51] Yet the writings of various leaders of the established order, including Timothy Dwight, reveal that the millennialism of their grandparents still formed a piece of their theological understanding of the United States.[52] Perhaps that millennialism now proved visionary rather than immanent.

That immanent sense of millennialism did, to a certain degree, find a home both in the revivalist groups and in the various schools of thought often referred to as Deism.

> The deist tradition . . . among moderns included Volney, . . . Godwin and sometimes Joel Barlow. The central tenet of this kind of deism was the perfectability of man . . . . The new religion, teaching the goodness of man and God, would be as simple and understandable as it was benign.

And it would use themes very similar to Puritan millennialism.[53]

The established clergy did not see the deists as descendents of their Puritan ancestors and opposed their influence over American minds. They were not united in their theology and practice of opposition, however, just as their ancestors had been divided among themselves.

The major division among those who remained Congregationalists has been called many names, but most often "New Divinity" vs. "Old Divinity." The two groups bear some resemblance to New

---

50. Morgan, "Puritan Ethic," 197.

51. Bonomi, *Cope*, 7.

52. See, for example, Dwight's poem *Greenfield Hill*, published in 1794, which ends in a vision of the future of America as God's realm beyond all the corruption of both Europe and "the East." *The Major Poems of Timothy Dwight*, William McTaggart and William Bottorff, eds. (Gainesville, Florida: Scholars' Facsimiles and Reprints, 1969), 367–542.

53. May, *Enlightenment*, 231–32.

Light/Old Light, but the politics are a bit more complicated, and the theology revolves around differing interpretations of Jonathan Edwards' theology and ethics. Timothy Dwight and the Yale leadership aligned with the New Divinity camp, a movement that reached its apex after Dwight with Nathaniel Taylor in what is known as New Haven Theology.

Despite Dwight's and the New Divinity's abhorrence of the rationalism of the deists, their reading of Edwards' theology involved a more humanistic, reason-centered bent.

> The being of God was considered above all else. But humanity and its happiness became more pivotal to God's glory than they had been. . . . Disinterested benevolence showed the movement of Congregationalists away from a mysterious divine cosmos to a human-centered one, just as the theology itself relied less on mystery and more on what appeared reasonable for divines to believe. . . . The New Divinity emphasized Edwards' notion of the deity's moral government; God was a constitutional monarch who ruled according to law. . . . The governed were a social order of accountable beings. The divine law promised rewards and punishments. God's administration was ever just.[54]

Like the deists, adherents to the New Divinity were criticized for being "arid and scholastic."[55]

In addition to the deists and the legally established churches, a major force during and after the revolution were the newer religious groups. Henry May characterizes the state of American organized religion on the eve of the revolution as consisting of two major camps: "the camp of folk religion and that of intellectual Calvinism." By folk religion, he means Baptists, Methodists, Separatists, and a variety of other, smaller groups. May observes that "in the democratic future, the victory was to go to this camp, which flourished in the time of crisis and knew how to touch the hearts of the people."

Until the nineteeth century, Calvinism and the Congregational churches had the organization, the money, the brains and the power[56] to dominate New England religious thought. But by the end of the eighteenth century, the Congregational churches faced a steady membership drain, partially attributable to these groups, that perplexed the educated urban clergy. In 1776, the Congregationalists and Presbyterians together could claim nearly forty percent of the American population as adherents. By 1850, their share had

---

54. Kuklick, *Churchmen*, 53 and 61.
55. Ibid., 64.
56. May, *Enlightenment*, 61.

fallen to less than sixteen percent, with the Methodists and Baptists (the more populist churches) making up more than half of the population.[57]

> In the wake of the revolution, dissenters confounded the establishment with an approach to theological matters that was nothing short of guerilla warfare. The coarse language, earthy humor, biting sarcasm, and commonsense reasoning of their attacks appealed to the uneducated but left the professional clergy without a ready defense. The very ground rules of religious life were at stake.[58]

Hatch speculates that this class conflict—based on levels of education and social standing rather than actual wealth—hit the churches harder than legal disestablishment.[59] It certainly struck a theological blow to a group who conceived of God as one who carefully ordered creation, and who is revealed as much in that order as anywhere else.

Even before disestablishment, laws in both Connecticut and Massachusetts allowed for dissenters from the Congregational churches (see above), but the label "dissenters" reveals the attitude of the leadership of the Congregational churches toward other faith expressions. As long as these groups remained a minority, their threat to the established order proved minimal. Once their numbers increased, and their attacks joined with the attacks of a free press, Congregational clergy assumed a defensive posture. Indeed, they went on the offense against the spread of "dissent." Thus arises the controversy over the origins of the Second Great Awakening.

Many scholars attribute the early days of this revival to political maneuvering on the part of Timothy Dwight and the Standing Order in Connecticut.

> [The Second Great Awakening] was not a spontaneous upwelling of faith, but a calculated endeavor, planned and executed by conservative evangelicals . . . . Connecticut became the center of confrontation between latter day Puritans and democratic insurgents. Out of this battle came an elaborate apology for the traditional faith and culture of New England. Its chief architect was Timothy Dwight.[60]

In a supporting opinion, Bruce Kuklick goes so far as to say that Dwight "hoped the revivals would arrest democratic change, com-

---

57. Mark Noll, *A History of Christianity in the United States and Canada* (Grand Rapids: Eerdmans, 1992), 153. While any statistics on this period are problematic as previously noted, the trend is fairly clear.

58. Hatch, *Democratization*, 34.

59. Ibid., 35.

60. Berk, *Calvinism*, x, 5.

bat ecclesiastic formalism and ultimately result in a conservative evangelical polity."[61]

If that was Dwight's hope as he entered the presidency of Yale in 1795 and sought to transform the religious life of the students, he was disappointed. The revivals of the next forty years or so went far beyond New England, far beyond Congregationalism, and perhaps promoted rather than arrested democratic change in both nation and churches.

In contrast to Berk, Kuklick, Mead, and others, Richard Birdsall and Richard Shiels see the genesis of the Awakening not in politics or polity, not even in Yale, but in the changes in the social order of the nation at the time.[62] Although Shiels admits that the early leaders of the Awakening were all Federalist clergy, and that "in such a setting, the new awakening must have been colored by political issues and alignments,"[63] following Birdsall, he sees the Awakening coming much more from the search by the people for a vibrant faith enabling more personal expression and from the spread of the missionary impulse after the revolution. Hatch noted that

> People nursed at least four related complaints against Reformed orthodoxy: its implicit endorsement of the status quo, its tyranny over personal religious experience, its preoccupation with complicated and arcane dogma, and its clerical pretension and quest for control.[64]

Although the Second Great Awakening manifested itself in many established churches and at Yale, as had its predecessor, it found its great home as the nineteenth century progressed, in the "dissenting" churches: Methodists, Baptists, the newly emerging Disciples of Christ, and on the frontier, rather than in the urban centers of Massachusetts and Connecticut where that clerical control was strongest. If Dwight hoped for a conservative victory out of the Awakening, what he saw was common people staking a claim on their own religious experience. And that religious experience did not always fit the model of New Divinity Calvinism.

The Great Awakening influenced politics and polity, certainly, but it also changed the worship life of the established churches. Clear evidence of this appears in preaching, but just as clearly it

---

61. Kuklick, *Churchmen*, 95.

62. Richard Birdsall,"The Second Great Awakening and the New England Social Order" *Church History* 39 (1970): 345–64. Richard Shiels, "The Second Great Awakening in Connecticut: Critique of the Traditional Interpretation" *Church History* 49 (1980): 401–15.

63. Shiels, "The Second Great Awakening in Connecticut," 411.

64. Hatch, *Democratization*, 171.

appears in the song of the church. As noted above, the second half
of the eighteenth century saw a considerable change in how worshipers sang in public worship. From a small selection of Psalm
tunes and a strictly translated set of words drawn only from the
Psalms of the Bible, worshipers began to sing, without first having
them lined out by a precentor, more diverse tunes and more diverse
words. William Billings and other musical entrepreneurs opened
their "singing schools" and wrote dozens of books with new tunes
in new musical styles, and the volunteer choir appeared in some
churches.[65] Music grew in quality and importance in the churches,
and some even introduced instruments to accompany singing. As
the quote from Bonomi above (see note 48) indicates, people owned
and used Psalters and hymnals for their own devotional reading and
family worship. Singing rose again as a central part of the lives of
Christians in worship and at home, out of a time when tunes had
been forgotten and singing seemed more a duty than a delight.
Hatch comments

> In short, eighteenth-century evangelicals—the Watts, Whitefields, and
> Wesleys, men of proper learning and character—struggled to reorient
> an elitist communications structure in their quest to infuse the gospel
> with new meaning and purpose for ordinary people.[66]

Although the essential format of worship at the end of the eighteenth century differed little from the beginning of the century, the
evolution of style and content reflected some of the myriad changes
going on socially, politically, and theologically. By 1800, the established New England Congregational churches could no longer claim
to be at the center of life in the villages and cities of the new nation,
even if their meeting houses still stood on the town greens. Buffeted
by what the clergy perceived as political threats from home and
abroad, theological threats from both within and outside the Congregational ranks, and social threats from the changing class system
and the growing, diverse population, the leadership of the churches
found many avenues of response. Many took their concerns to
newspapers and journals, founding new ones when the established
avenues of communication seemed hostile. Many preached and lec-
tured. Some ran for political office, though that was a more common
phenomenon in Massachusetts than Connecticut.[67] Some looked

---

65. Rochelle A. Stackhouse, "Hymns of Love and Praise: A Brief History of Music in American Congregational Churches," *Prism* 8 (Spring
1993): 43.

66. Hatch, *Democratization*, 128.

67. Baldwin, *New England Clergy*, 137.

within the life of the church, within the worship of the church, and specifically within the song of the church, to express their concerns, hopes, beliefs, and fears about the new nation in formation. For some, this meant a divergence from the old Psalm-singing tradition of the descendents of the Puritans, as the rage for hymn-writing and singing emerged in the wake of Watts and the Wesleys. But for others, the Psalms themselves provided an opportunity to reflect on and communicate about the role of the church in the new world. We turn now to the tradition of the Psalms in worship to explore the final context in which Watts, Mycall, Barlow, and Dwight dwelt.

Chapter Three

Psalms Reformed

History of Psalmody

Throughout the early history of Christianity, writers catalog Psalm-singing among believers, as the words of David, Asaph, and the other Psalmists of Israel took on new meaning for the followers of Jesus.[1] Psalmody continued to hold a place of honor in worship throughout the medieval church, but only choirs actually sang the Psalms (to Gregorian Psalm tones), exclusively in Latin. One of the many contributions the Reformation made to liturgy was to give the music of the church back to the whole congregation, and into their languages. Martin Luther and others wrote hymns and metrical Psalms to teach and inspire their congregations, and those in the Calvinist track of the Reformation enriched this practice of metrical Psalmody. Watts and his revisers find their roots in this practice, the only form of church song approved for public worship by Calvin and his descendants. "We cannot find better or more appropriate songs for this purpose," wrote Calvin, "than the Psalms of David, which the Holy Spirit himself has dictated and composed."[2]

Calvin and Clement Marot, a court poet, compiled the first metrical Psalter in Strasbourg in 1539.[3] Metrical Psalmody differs from hymnody or other forms of Psalmody in that the Psalms are trans-

---

1. For an excellent summary of psalm-singing in the early churches, see the brief article by Mary Berry in *The New Westminster Dictionary of Liturgy and Worship*, ed. J. G. Davies (Philadelphia: Westminster, 1986), 450.

2. Cited in Davies, *The Worship of the American Puritans*, 49 n59.

3. For an excellent summary of the history and concept of Metrical Psalters, see the brief article by Erik Routley in *Key Words in Church Music*, ed. Carl Schalk (St. Louis: Concordia, 1978), 250. For a more extensive treatment of the subject, see Robin A. Leaver, *'Goostly Psalmes and Spirituall Songs': English and Dutch Metrical Psalms from Coverdale to Utenhove 1535-1566* (Oxford: Clarendon Press, 1991).

lated into the vernacular in strophic form, to fit a specific meter. The translation does not seek total accuracy or even poetic beauty, but rather ease of congregational singing.

Though Calvin's Psalter (both the Strasbourg version of 1539 and the famous Genevan Psalter of 1562 edited by Louis Bourgeois) was in French, English attempts at this metrical Psalmody quickly followed. Myles Coverdale's *Goostly Psalmes and Spirituall Songs* appeared as early as 1535, but Henry VIII banned it and it disappeared before gaining wide usage. Political changes allowed Thomas Sternhold to begin a Psalter not long before his death in 1549. John Hopkins and colleagues eventually completed this work in 1562.

The Whole Booke of Psalms,[4] more commonly known as Sternhold and Hopkins, or the "Old Version," proved extremely popular in English churches. Various independent clergy and lay poets tried their hand at the art, but none had the impact of Sternhold and Hopkins until Nahum Tate and Nicholas Brady published what was popularly known as the "New Version" in 1696. While Sternhold and Hopkins' Psalms had been fairly close translations from the Hebrew, Tate and Brady made the first step toward hymnody in styling looser translations which were more easily sung by congregations.[5] Many protested this loosening of standards and the New Version—though ultimately extremely influential on the future of English-speaking church song—never gained the hearts and minds of worshipers as had Sternhold and Hopkins, especially in the rural churches.

The earliest English-speaking group to come to New England, the Pilgrims, brought with them one of the independent productions that followed the French-Genevan model more consistently than Sternhold and Hopkins: the Ainsworth Psalter.[6] Written by an Englishman living in the Netherlands, it, like earlier English Psalters, kept a fairly literal standard of translation, resulting in rather rough poetry but with more varied meters than most English Psalters, reflecting the influence of the numerous French-German tunes it employed. Psalm-singing was a central part of public worship and private devotion for the Pilgrims. At the departure of the Pilgrims for America from the Netherlands, Edward Winslow remembered, "Wee refreshed ourselves after our teares with singing of Psalmes . . . there being many of the Congregation very expert in Musick."[7]

---

4. Thomas Sternhold and John Hopkins, *The Whole Booke of Psalms collected into English Metre* (London: John Day, 1562).

5. Louis Benson, *The English Hymn* (Richmond: John Knox 1915), 50ff.

6. Henry Ainsworth, *The Booke of Psalmes Englished both in Prose and Metre* (Amsterdam: Thomas Stafford, 1612).

7. Cited in Zoltan Haraszti, *The Enigma of the Bay Psalm Book* (Chicago: University of Chicago Press, 1956), v.

The other Calvinist settlers of New England, the English Puritans/Independents, came not with Ainsworth, but with Sternhold and Hopkins and Thomas Ravenscroft's 1621 Psalter, which included the texts from the Old Version, but with four-part settings of the English Psalm tunes and some new tunes.[8]

The Bay Psalm Book

The English Puritans who traveled to America did so primarily to establish a place for what they considered "pure" worship and theology. Part of that desire for purity included a zeal for absolutely literal translations of scripture for use in worship. Although Sternhold and Hopkins did not stray far from the scriptures when measured against modern hymns or Psalm paraphrases, Puritan leaders in New England felt their translations were somewhat loose. Within ten years of the establishment of the Puritans in New England, John Cotton, Richard Mather, Thomas Weld, and John Eliot (among others) translated, versified, and published the first edition of the Bay Psalm Book or *The Whole Book of Psalms Faithfully Translated into English Metre*, the first complete book published in the colonies.[9]

The preface, thought to be written either by Richard Mather or John Cotton, divulges the thoughts of the editors on the matter of translation:

> wee have therefore done our indeavour to make a plaine and familiar translation of the Psalmes and words of David into english metre, and have not soe much as presumed to paraphrase to give the sense of his meaning in other words; we have therefore attended heerin as our chief guide the originall, shunning all additions, except such as even the best translators of them in prose supply . . . .[10]

---

8. Thomas Ravenscroft, *The whole Book of Psalmes, with the Hymns Evangelicall and Songs Spirituall, composed into 4 parts by sundry Authors, with several tunes as have beene and are usually sung in England, Scotland, Wales, Germany, Italy, France, and the Netherlands, never as yet before in one volume published*, 1621.

9. Much of the material on the Bay Psalm Book comes from Haraszti. See also *A Facsimile Reprint of the First Edition of the Bay Psalm Book* (New York: Burt Franklin, 1973), bound together with a list of editions of the Bay Psalm Book, and George Parker Winship, *The Cambridge Press 1638-1692: A Reexamination of the Evidence Concerning the Bay Psalm Book and the Eliot Indian Bible* (Philadelphia: University of Pennsylvania Press, 1945).

10. Bay Psalm Book, sig.**2^v - **3^r.

Psalm 100 provides an interesting example in comparing the Bay Psalm Book to the English Psalters that preceded it. John Hopkins wrote a version of the Psalm, "In God the Lord by glad and light," which appeared in the 1562 edition of Sternhold and Hopkins, but subsequent editions returned to what had already become the standard English version of this Psalm: William Kethe's "All people that on earth do dwell."

1. All people that on earth do dwell
   Sing to the Lord with cheerful voice
   Him serve with fear, his praise forth tell
   Come ye before him and rejoice.

3. The Lord, ye know, is God indeed,
   Without our aide, he did us make:
   We are his flock, he doth us feed,
   And for his sheepe he doth us take.

4. O enter, then his gates with praise:
   Approach with joy his courts unto:
   Praise, laud and bless his Name always,
   For it is seemly so to do.

5. For why? The Lord our God is good,
   His mercy is for ever sure:
   His truth at all times firmly stood,
   And shall from age to age endure.[11]

The Bay Psalm Book, nearly a hundred years later, ignores Kethe's text and presents this version of Psalm 100:

Make ye a joyful sounding noise
unto Jehovah, all the earth:
Serve ye Jehovah with gladness:
Before his presence come with mirth.
Know that Jehovah he is God,
who hath us formed it is he,
and not ourselves: his own people
and sheep of his pasture are we.
Enter into his gates with praise,
into his Courts with thankfulness:
make ye confession unto him,
and his name reverently bless.
Because Jehovah he is good,
for evermore is his mercy:

---

11. Thomas Sternhold and John Hopkins, *The Whole Booke of Psalmes collected into English Meeter* (London: Company of Stationers, 1618).

and unto generations all
continue doth his verity.[12]

Clearly the Kethe is a less precise translation but much more easily
sung in meter than the awkward constructions of The Bay Psalm
Book.

The Puritan translations may have conformed literally to the
scriptures, but singing them proved difficult for many congregations. Cotton Mather's critical opinion summed up the problem: "a
little more Art was to be employ'd" upon it.[13] In 1647 a second
edition appeared, revised by Harvard president Henry Dunster and
Richard Lyon, that included more hymns such as the songs of Deb-
orah, Moses, Hannah, and various other canticles.

While Cotton Mather still felt it lacked "Art," the churches
adopted the revision enthusiastically. The New England Psalm
Book, as it came to be called, "was reprinted over fifty times during
the next hundred years," finding popularity equally in England and
Scotland.[14] It became the standard for New England churches—
despite other independent versions—until well into the eighteenth
century.

Isaac Watts

With the introduction of Tate and Brady's "New Version," a new
phase in the philosophy behind metrical Psalm translation/para-
phrases begins. Henry Wilder Foote notes that, though Tate and
Brady was still a fairly literal translation of the Psalms by modern
standards,

> Here and there the translation was tinged with the political coloring
> of the times. A congregation singing "The prince, who slights what
> God commands Exposed to scorn must quit his throne," could not
> fail to note the pointed reference to the dethronement and exile of
> James II, only eight years before the publication of the *New Version*.[15]

Before Tate and Brady, John Patrick published in 1679 *A Century
of Select Psalms and portions of the Psalms of David, especially those
of praise*. Patrick, for English-speaking churches, really began the

12. The Bay Psalm Book, sig. O^v -O1^r, 1640.

13. Haraszti, *Enigma*, 28.

14. Ibid., 29.

15. Henry Wilder Foote, *Three Centuries of American Hymnody* (Cambridge, Massachusetts: Harvard University Press, 1940), 37 n1.

move, as Benson puts it, to "accommodate the Scriptural text to the circumstances of present day worshipers,"[16] at least in terms of formal collections of Psalm texts meant for public worship. For some years, broadside ballads had presented hymn-like Psalms for public consumption commemorating such events as the defeat of the Spanish Armada (1588). Patrick's work found special welcome in the worship of the Nonconformists (for whom relevance was a major concern in liturgy), and, by Isaac Watts' own acknowledgment, formed a considerable influence on the young nonconformist from Southampton.[17]

Even before Patrick and Tate and Brady, the medieval Sarum Psalter had begun the process in England of interpreting the Psalms for Christian worship. Instead of changing the language of the Latin Psalms, the Sarum Psalter added hermeneutical subtitles, often interpreting the Psalms in the light of Jesus Christ. Watts actually used several of the Sarum subtitles in his work, and was clearly influenced by the method.[18]

Another major influence on young Watts concerned the actual practice of singing the Psalms in worship. While many clung to the more literal translations, the practice of lining out the Psalms meant that much of what was sung was incomprehensible. Lines of text were so broken up that no continuous thought remained. Therefore, the clerks who lined the Psalms and the clergy deleted verses to shorten the Psalm and left out some less popular Psalms altogether. Would it not be more practical to produce a Psalter more easily sung and understood and which did the cutting and deleting of Psalms ahead of time, in a more systematic and theologically sound form? According to Daggett, what Watts sought to do was to "change the *costume* of their [i.e., the Psalmists] thoughts, so as to make the songs themselves more appropriate and effective now."[19] That is, make them appropriate in language relevant to Christians and effective in a style more tailored to singing. Watts distinguished between *reading* the Psalms, which he understood as God speaking to us, and *singing* the Psalms, which he understood to be our words to

---

16. Benson, *The English Hymn*, 51.

17. As Watts notes in the preface to *The Psalms of David Imitated.* Horton Davies notes in his history of the English churches that a small group called the Particular Baptists also preceded Watts in loosening up the paraphrases of the Psalms for worship. Horton Davies, *Worship and Theology in England*, vol. 2 (Princeton: Princeton University Press, 1961), 135.

18. Harry Escott, *Isaac Watts Hymnographer* (London: Independent Press, 1962), 150–151.

19. O. E. Daggett, "The Psalms in Worship," *The New Englander*, July 1846, 314.

God.[20] He believed that "a congregation would never sing tolerably well if the Psalms and hymns provided for its use were unintelligible and foreign to its experience."[21]

Isaac Watts, son of a strong nonconformist who was jailed more than once for his beliefs, began his quest to change how England's churchgoers sang as early as age twenty when he complained to his father about the rough singing in the Above Bar Independent church in Southampton. His father told young Isaac, who had written poetry since childhood, that if he did not like it, he should try to do better.[22] Six years later, his brother Enoch wrote to Isaac, complaining of the "New Version" of Tate and Brady:

> There is in them a mighty deficiency of that life and soul which is necessary to raise our fancies and kindle and fire our passions. I have been persuaded to a great while since, that were David to speak English he would choose to make use of your style.[23]

With this family backing and a supportive congregation at the Mark Lane chapel in London where he pastored, Watts set about developing his "System of Praise." In 1707 Watts published both "A short essay toward the improvement of Psalmody" and the first edition of *Hymns and Spiritual Songs*. Both in the Essay and in the Preface to *Hymns* Watts describes his plan for improving the singing in English-speaking churches. The basic plan included two parts: an "accommodation" of the Psalms to use in the Christian Church, and the development of an "evangelical hymnody" to supplement the Psalms with hymns appropriate to events not found in the Psalms (i.e., Holy Communion, life of Christ, the Church).[24]

In 1719, with the publication of *The Psalms of David Imitated in the Language of the New Testament*, Watts completed his System. He "imitated" 138 of the Psalms, feeling that 12 of the Psalms proved unsuitable for singing by Christians, along with some parts

---

20. "By reading we learn what God speaks to us in his Word; but when we sing . . . our chief Design is or should be to speak our own Hearts and our Words to God"; Isaac Watts, *Hymns and Spiritual Songs with an Essay towards the Improvement of Christian Psalmody by the Use of Evangelical Hymns in Worship as well as the Psalms of David* (London: J. Humphreys, 1707), 243.

21. Escott, *Isaac Watts*, 115.

22. David Fountain, *Isaac Watts Remembered* (Worthing: Henry Walter, 1974), 34.

23. Ibid., 53.

24. Watts, "An Essay Toward the Improvement . . . ," 246ff.

of the 138 Psalms he did include.[25] His preface describes his design as:

> *To accomodate the Book of Psalms to Christian Worship*: And in order
> to do this 'tis necessary to divest *David and Asaph*, etc. of every other
> character but that of a *Psalmist and a Saint, and to make them always
> speak the common sense and language of a Christian.*[26]

Clearly Watts had made the move to a new hermeneutic of metrical Psalmody. "In the older metrical versions there was the concern for a re-presentation of the Psalm, but in Watts the concern was for reinterpretation."[27]

Part of Watts' goal with this book was to remedy one of the problems he found in Southampton as a young man: to make the Psalms more singable. His "imitations" reflect a more poetic, less literal style. For example, Watts' version of Psalm 100, 2nd meter, reads:

Sing to the Lord with joyful voice;
Let every land his name adore;
The British Isles shall send the Noise
Across the Ocean to the Shore.

Nations attend before his Throne
With solemn Fear, with sacred Joy;
Know that the Lord is God alone;
He can create, and he destroy.

His soveriegn Power without our Aid
Made us of Clay, and formed us Men:
And when like wandering sheep we strayed
He brought us to his fold again.

We are his People, we his care,
Our Souls and all our mortal Frame:
What lasting Honours shall we rear
Almighty Maker, to thy Name.

---

25. The missing 12 include the strongest of the imprecatory Psalms: 28, 43, 52, 54, 59, 64, 70, 79, 88, 108, 137, 140. In his "Essay Towards the Improvement . . ." of 1707 cited above, Watts notes: "Yet you will always find in this Paraphrase dark Expressions enlightened and the Levitical ceremonies and Hebrew forms of Speech changed into the Worship of the Gospel, and explained in the Language of our Time and Nation; and what would not bear such an Alteration is omitted and laid aside," x.

26. *The Psalms of David Imitated*, 1719, xvi.

27. Robin A. Leaver, "Isaac Watts' Hermeneutical Principles and the Decline of English Metrical Psalmody," *Churchman* 92 (1978): 58.

We'll crowd thy Gates with thankful Songs,
High as the Heavens our Voices raise:
And Earth with her ten thousand Tongues
Shall fill thy courts with sounding Praise.

Wide as the World is thy command,
Vast as Eternity thy Love;
Firm as a Rock thy truth must stand
When rolling years shall cease to move.

Compare this version to that of Kethe or the Bay Psalm Book above and the change Watts brought becomes clear.

Watts also made, as his System indicated, David and Asaph, etc. speak as English subjects. Foote goes so far as to interpret Watts' use of specifically English references as " 'accommodating' the Psalms to make them a mouthpiece for British patriotism."[28] In fact often, though not always, when a Biblical Psalm made reference to the nation of Israel or "Zion," Watts substituted a reference to his native land. This was an important contribution at a time in which British identity as a nation, including its religious identity, was in a state of flux. From the Restoration of the Monarchy and the Church in 1660, to the coming of William and Mary and the Toleration Act (giving non-conformists like Watts new legitimacy), to the establishment of the Hanoverian line in 1714, questions of church and state and the identity of both occupied the minds of many Britons. As his American revisers would do later, Watts used the occasion of public singing of the Psalms to contribute to these discussions.

Obviously Watts' hermeneutic of the Psalter allowed him to understand that the Psalms themselves had originally been composed for very specific situations of life contemporary to their authors. Indeed, the superscription for Psalms such as 51, 52, 56, 57, and others make those specific references clear to subsequent singers. Watts' understanding of himself not as a translator per se, but as an imitator or interpreter, compelled him to compose metrical Psalms that spoke to the lives of the people who sang them. Therefore, the words had to be clearly understood. He emphasized the identity of the singers as Christians, and English Christians specifically, and considered the current political and social situation as he wrote. Indeed, one of Watts' recent biographers notes that the paraphrase of Psalm 90, "Our God Our Help in Ages Past," was written at the time of the Schism Bill when dissenters from the Church of England (such as Watts and his family) once again faced persecution.[29] Watts

---

28. Henry Wilder Foote, *Three Centuries of American Hymnody*, 37.
29. Fountain, *Watts Remembered*, 65.

himself made several of these situations clear, as his superscription to Psalm 60 indicates: "On a Day of Humiliation for Disappointments in War," or Psalm 115, which reads, "A Psalm for the Fifth of November," (the date of the Gunpowder Plot; Guy Fawkes Day). In his "Essay Toward the Improvement . . .," Watts cites as his example the New Testament use of the Psalms in revised form. He notes specifically Acts 4:23–26 where, in the King James Version, the disciples sing a slightly revised form of the second Psalm which includes a reference to David singing about Christ.[30] In this Watts expressed his clear Puritan heritage, believing that "like spoken prayer, praise had to do with the present experience and needs of the worshipper."[31]

Setting this model of the Psalms sung in worship reflecting the situation of the people who sing them practically requires that subsequent generations would revise Watts to make sense in their own times and places, or even write new Psalms and hymns themselves. In Great Britain, but more quickly in the British Colonies in America and later the United States, this revising and composing took place even before Watts' death in 1748.

John Wesley: First Reviser in the American Context

Before *The Psalms of David Imitated* was published in England, Watts sent samples to Cotton Mather in Massachusetts for his consideration, especially Psalm 107, which Watts entitled "A Psalm for New England."[32] Clearly Watts had the American market in mind. Almost certainly Watts had a copy of the revised Bay Psalm Book, so he knew the type of Psalm singing current in New England churches. He also knew the controversy engendered by the debate over the degeneration of singing in the churches, a product of both precentors (those who lined out the Psalms in worship) and congregations having lost the communal memory of Psalm tunes. To combat this, many advocated singing "the regular way," with congregations able to sing as one without lining out by a precen-

---

30. Watts, "An Essay Towards the Improvement . . .," 252.

31. Escott, *Isaac Watts*, 115.

32. For a fascinating look at two of the great minds of their times, see the correspondence of Isaac Watts to Cotton Mather preserved in the *Proceedings of the Massachusetts Historical Society*, IX (Boston: The Society, 1879), 368ff. The letters show a considerable exchange of books and ideas across the Atlantic between the two men.

tor.[33] Watts supported "the regular way." The first American reprint of his Psalter, however, did not appear until Benjamin Franklin published it in 1729, though Franklin notes that it sat on his shelves largely unsold.[34] In 1741, the first Boston edition from the press of Rogers and Fowle issued. Although slow to catch on until after the American revolution, the Great Awakening and the influence of Whitefield and Jonathan Edwards, as well as the growing success of the "regular singing" party, moved the preferences of New England congregations beyond the stilted metrical translation of Bay Psalm.

Before the first Boston printing, however, John Wesley introduced Watts' *Psalms of David Imitated* and some of Watts' hymns to the nascent Methodist movement. In 1737 at Charleston, South Carolina, Wesley had printed his *Collection of Psalms and Hymns*.[35] Although Wesley does not identify authorship of any of the Psalms and hymns in the book, comparison with Watts' 1719 Psalter shows Wesley's use of Watts' versions of 14 Psalm imitations, as well as numerous hymns by Watts.[36] Wesley revised almost every one of these borrowed Psalms, however. In some cases, such as 51, 65, and 147, Wesley simply left out some of Watts' verses and added one or two of unknown composition. In most instances the missing verses are those Watts presented in brackets to indicate they were optional. In several places, Wesley changed Watts' text, including specific references to the British Isles. For example, the fourth verse of Psalm 19, short meter, first part, in Watts reads:

Ye British lands rejoice
Where he reveals his Word:
We are not left to Nature's voice
To bid us know the Lord.

Wesley changes the first line to read:

Ye happy lands rejoice.

---

33. This singing controversy dominated many musical discussions in churches of the eighteenth century. See chapter five.

34. Benson, *The English Hymn*, 162.

35. *Collection of Psalms and Hymns* (Charleston: Lewis Timothy), 1737. Facsimile copy from Nashville: The United Methodist Publishing House, 1988.

36. See the essay "The Sources of John Wesley's 'Collection of Psalms and Hymns,' Charleston, 1737" in *John Wesley's First Hymn-Book*, Frank Baker and George Williams, eds. (London: Wesley Historical Society, 1964), xxvii–xxviv. The Psalm imitations included are Psalms 19 (two parts), 33, 38, 47, 51, 65, 90 (two parts), 100, 114, 146, 147, and 148.

Similarly, in Psalm 47, verse 6, line 1, Watts writes:

The British Islands are the Lord's;

while Wesley's version reads:

Remotest Nations are the Lord's.

In the case of Psalm 38, Wesley's changes appear to be aesthetic. For example, the first line of verse 3 in Watts reads:

My Sins a heavy load appear,

while in Wesley's version the same line, now the second verse of the Psalm, reads:

My Sins a heavy Burden are.

Four other lines in this Psalm show minor changes from Watts to Wesley.

Psalm 146 also reflects aesthetic changes, which appear in the first two lines of Watts' fourth verse, Wesley's third. Watts writes:

The Lord hath eyes to give the blind;
The Lord supports the sinking mind,

while Wesley revises the lines to read:

The Lord pours Eye-sight on the Blind,
The Lord supports the fainting Mind.

Carlton Young determined that one of the reasons for Wesley's revisions had to do with meter. Wesley changed all the Psalms and hymns in this book into six meters to enhance their singability. That alone required some aesthetic changes.[37] The metrical changes, however, do not account for all of Wesley's revisions. In a hymnal meant as much for British as for American churches, long before the colonies fought for an identity separate from "British lands,"[38] Wesley made the first move toward making Watts' language more universal,

---

37. Carlton Young, "John Wesley's 1737 Charlestown *Collection of Psalms and Hymns*," *The Hymn* 41 (October 1990): 23.

38. Indeed, Wesley printed a revised version of the *Collection* in 1738 in London.

less specific to time and place, though maintaining his style of "imitation" rather than direct translation.

Watts' Progress in New England

The first reprints of both Watts' *Psalms of David Imitated* and his *Hymns and Spiritual Songs*[39] reached New England as Whitefield and Edwards and others led what is now known as the First Great Awakening.[40] However, most parishes, as opposed to revival meetings, did not adopt Watts wholesale until much nearer the time of the revolution and especially after it. "Apart from the prejudice of many against hymns and their affection for *The Bay Psalm Book*, the free character of Watts' Imitations and his omission of several Psalms told against it."[41] In addition, Watts had competition in many churches from the "less free" rendering of Tate and Brady.[42] Several churches, such as Old South Church in Boston, Massachusetts, used the Bay Psalm Book with supplements of hymns by Watts, or Tate and Brady with a similar supplement. Some churches, such as South Church in Portsmouth, New Hampshire, used Watts' Psalms without the hymns.[43] But it was not until after the revolution, and especially after the revisions discussed below, that both the Psalms and hymns of Watts found wide usage in the New England Congregational churches.

---

39. In later editions and revisions, often titled *Psalms and Hymns*, the Psalm paraphrases and the Hymns were bound together. See Selma Bishop, *Isaac Watts's Hymns and Spiritual Songs (1707): A Publishing History and A Bibliography* (Ann Arbor: The Pierian Press, 1974).

40. Jonathan Edwards notes in a letter dated May 22, 1744, that his congregation had been using Watts' hymns in the summer "for more than two years past"; *Proceedings of the Massachusetts Historical Society*, X (Boston: The Society, 1896), 429.

41. Benson, *The English Hymn*, 164.

42. In a letter from Watts to Cotton Mather in January of 1740, he wonders how anyone could criticize his selection of the Psalms and "be zealous" for Sternhold and Hopkins or Tate and Brady over his version; see *Proceedings*, IX, 369.

43. Benson, *The English Hymn*, 165.

Chapter Four

Reformation of the Reformed: Mycall, Barlow, and Dwight

John Mycall

Even before the American revolution, New Englanders were busy "naming, languaging and storying" their world in different ways than their English compatriots–or their predecessors in America. As early as 1752, The Rev. John Barnard of Marblehead, Massachusetts, sought to update church music to fit the times. He published *A New Version of the Psalms Fitted to the Tunes used in the Churches with Several Hymns out of the Old and New Testament.* In the preface he wrote:

> Though the New England Version of the Psalms of David in Metre [i.e., the revised version of the Bay Psalm Book] is generally very good, and few of the same Age may be compar'd with it; yet the flux of Languages has rendered several phrases in it obsolete, and the Mode of Expression in various Places less acceptable: for which Reasons an Amendment, or New Version has been long, and greatly desired, by the most judicious among us.[1]

Unfortunately for Barnard's sales, by this time the churches were beginning to explore the Watts' Psalms and hymns, but his effort makes clear that the market existed for a Psalter more suited to the times and the changes in the English language.

Others followed his lead, but not in revising the Bay Psalm Book. As Watts caught on in the churches during the revolutionary period, the market for Psalters in the churches demanded more singable Psalm imitations, like Watts', and not exact translations. Amazingly,

---

1. Henry Wilder Foote, *Three Centuries of American Hymnody* (Cambridge, Massachusetts: Harvard University Press, 1940), 156.

even with all the overt references to matters British, the original version of Watts continued to be printed in this country during and after the revolution and was used by some churches.[2]

But in New England, it soon became clear that

> To make the Imitations palatable at that epoch to the newly won liberties of America, some changes were necesary in those passages in which Watts had made David appear as a patriotic Englishman. Outside of Connecticut these changes were made without common action of the churches, under the auspices of private printers.[3]

The earliest of these private versions for which any strong record exists was published in 1781, before the final treaty ending the revolution, by John Mycall in Newburyport, Massachusetts. Little information about Mycall remains beyond his basic biography. Born in Worcester, England, Mycall was educated to be a school teacher, and after coming to New England, he kept a school at Newburyport and also taught at Amesbury, Massachusetts.[4] By 1776, he went into partnership with Henry Tinges in a printing house in Newburyport originally started by Isaiah Thomas in 1773. After six months, Mycall bought out Tinges and continued alone for 20 years.[5] The major publication was *The Essex Journal and Merrimack Packet*, a newspaper of some local note. Buckingham's evaluation of Mycall as newspaper editor falls short of praise; he writes that after the paper fell solely into Mycall's hands, "it is rare to meet with an editorial paragraph of any merit, or a communication worthy of notice."[6] Apparently after twenty years of such unmeritorious service, Mycall retired to a farm near Cambridge where he died either in 1826 (Buckingham) or 1833 (Thomas).

---

2. Benson notes that an unaltered edition of Watts was published in Philadelphia in 1781 by Robert Aitken, a patriot who appears to have "suffered at the hands of the British army." Benson expresses surprise that such a person would print Watts unaltered. One assumes he did so because a market existed and no widely accepted alteration had yet been attempted. Louis Benson, "The American Revisions of Watts's 'Psalms' " in *Journal of the Presbyterian Historical Society* II (1903–04): 19.

3. Benson, *The English Hymn* (Philadelphia: The Presbyterian Board of Publications, 1915), 166.

4. Biographical data on Mycall comes from Isaiah Thomas, *The History of Printing in America* (Barre, Mass: Imprint Society, 1970 reprint of 1810 original), 179–291, and from Joseph Buckingham, *Specimens of Newspaper Literature*, Vol. I (Freeport, NY: Books for Libraries Press, 1971 reprint of 1850 original), 298–303.

5. Thomas, *History of Printing*, 179.

6. Buckingham, *Specimens*, 303.

In addition to the newspaper, in 1781, Mycall published *The Psalms of David, Imitated in the Language of the New Testament, and applied to the Christian State and Worship. By I. Watts, D.D. The fortieth edition, corrected, and accommodated to the use of the Church of Christ in America.* Fortunately for Mycall's sales, a New England leader with the stature of the President of Yale, Ezra Stiles, had fonder praise for this book than Buckingham had for Mycall's editorials. Stiles noted the publication in his diary entry for December 8, 1781:

> This year has been published the fourtieth Edition of Dr. Watts's Psalms: it was printed at Newburyport in Massachusetts by Mr. Mycall, Printer. He with the Advice and Assist of neighboring ministers and others has made some Alterations in Psalms where G. Britain is mentioned, and references to the King of Gt. Britain–as in the 75th Psalm. At first it may seem as if these alterations were many: however they really are but few. Thus the Ps. Book is well adapted to the Chh in America.[7]

The next chapter will explore the changes in the Mycall version in some detail, but Stiles' assessment misses the mark in terms of the number of changes. Most of the significant changes did have to do with British references, but Mycall also made some aesthetic and grammatical alterations, perhaps in line with language differences between 1719 England and 1781 New England.

Stiles' approval may have had some influence in the use of the book, as at least five subsequent editions were published, and not by Mycall himself. Benson catalogues editions published in 1787 by Peter Edes of Boston, 1789 by John Folsom of Boston, 1802, 1804, and 1812 by Merriam of Brookfield, Massachusetts, these last four bound together with Watts' *Hymns.*[8] Unfortunately, no record remains of who the "neighboring ministers" were whom Stiles noted in his diary.

Joel Barlow

Obviously if Ezra Stiles obtained a copy of Mycall's revision of Watts, churches in both Massachusetts and Connecticut also had access to the book. They would have added it to the numerous Psalters in use at the time, including The Bay Psalm Book, Sternhold

---

7. *The Literary Diary of Ezra Stiles,* Vol. 2 (New York: Scribner's Sons, 1901), 571.

8. Benson, "The American Revisions," 21.

and Hopkins, Tate and Brady, Watts' *Psalms of David Imitated* un-revised, and Watts' *Hymns and Spiritual Songs.*

While Massachusetts clergy may not have considered the variety of music being sung in the Congregational churches as problematic, Connecticut organized its churches more tightly. The General Association of Connecticut exercised a centralized control over such matters as accepting candidates for the ministry and disciplining clergy. Today one might describe Connecticut's ecclesiastical organization as more "presbyterian" in nature than truly "congregational." In 1784, the General Association considered this lack of uniformity in the churches' song, and made a commission recorded in Barlow's revision:

> that a number of Psalms in Doctor Watts's version, which are locally appropriated, should be altered and applied to the state of the Christian Church in general, and not to any particular country; and finding some attempts had been made to alter and apply those Psalms to America, or particular parts of America [re. Mycall], tending to destroy that uniformity in the use of Psalmody, so desireable in religious assemblies; they appointed the Rev. Messrs. Timothy Pitkin, John Smally and Theodore Hinsdale, a Committee to confer with and apply to Mr. Joel Barlow, of Hartford, to make the proposed alterations.[9]

"Mr. Joel Barlow of Hartford," with his partner Elisha Babcock, ran a publishing house in 1784 which printed the newspaper *The American Mercury* as well as books and pamphlets. His career both before and after his year-long stint as a publisher is considerably more varied and central to American history than that of John Mycall.

Barlow, the fourth child of farmers Samuel and Esther Barlow of Redding, Connecticut, was born the year Jonathan Edwards published "The Freedom of the Will," 1754.[10] A bright student from a family of little means, he obtained a scholarship to Moors Indian School, the preparatory school for Dartmouth college. After his fa-

---

9. This note is included on the first page of Barlow's first edition, Hartford: Barlow and Babcock, 1785.

10. Barlow's life has been explored in several books, including Theodore Zunder, *The Early Days of Joel Barlow a Connecticut Wit* (New Haven: 1934); Charles Burr Todd, *Life and Letters of Joel Barlow, LLD* (New York: Putnam's, 1886); James L. Woodress, *A Yankee's Odyssey: The Life of Joel Barlow* (Philadelphia: Lippincott, 1958). The Todd is as much hagiography as biography with the Woodress being the most balanced treatment of the three. Note also the books in the Bibliography concerning the Connecticut Wits.

ther's early death, he took his inheritance and transferred to Yale to complete his studies. At Yale he spent considerable time studying literature and poetry, new additions to the curriculum which had earlier been championed by Timothy Dwight and his contemporaries at Yale. Indeed, while at Yale Barlow conceived his desire to become a great American poet, and had an opportunity to begin this career by reading one of his own compositions, on a patriotic theme, at his commencement exercises in 1778.[11]

Barlow's college career coincided with the outbreak of war, and his time at Yale was disrupted briefly to serve in Washington's army on Long Island and the losing campaign for New York.[12] He returned to Yale to complete his degree, joining classmate Noah Webster. Along with historical and theological studies, Barlow, as Dwight before him, found Lord Kames' book *Elements of Criticism* influential on both his poetry and his philosophy. Kames' main principle was

> a conviction, that the common nature of man (sic) is invariable not less than universal, we conceive that it hath no relation to time nor to place; but that it will be the same hereafter as at present, and as it was in time past; the same among all nations.[13]

Having no clear future in mind, Barlow stayed at Yale for his master's degree, living with Timothy Dwight at Northampton and earning his way by working in Dwight's school there. Barlow at the time was working on his epic poem *The Vision of Columbus* as Dwight worked on his epic *The Conquest of Canaan*.

After his master's work, and still without prospects for a career, Barlow applied to the General Association of Connecticut to become a minister, as he had been promised a place as chaplain in the Army in 1780. He married Ruth Baldwin secretly, and traveled with the Fourth Massachusetts Brigade to New Jersey and the war.[14]

Earlier that year, Barlow had been introduced to David Humphreys, later part of the group of poets known as the "Connecticut Wits," which included Barlow. Humphreys was so impressed by what Barlow showed him of *Vision* in progress that he wrote to a friend in Boston:

---

11. Noted in Stiles, vol. II, 288. Stiles records that Barlow's poem was in English and took 12 minutes to read. The poem, "The Prospect of Peace," was later published.

12. Woodress, *Yankee's Odyssey*, 40.

13. Quoted in Leon Howard, *The Connecticut Wits* (Chicago: University of Chicago Press, 1943), 26–27.

14. Woodress, *Yankee's Odyssey*, 52ff; Zunder, *Early Days*, 105ff.

Barlow I saw, and here began
My friendship for that spotless man
Whom, though the world does not yet know it,
Great nature form'd her loftiest poet.[15]

Barlow's reputation as a literary figure owed a great deal at that early stage to influential and respected friends such as Dwight and Humphreys.

Barlow seems to have had a fairly easy time of his task as chaplain, including dining with General Washington at one event. His attitude toward the ministry indicated that the profession was decidedly temporary. After his second sermon, he wrote to Ruth, "Yesterday I had another preachment, which kept me awake awhile—whether it had the same effect upon others I am not certain."[16] Other letters to her carry a similar tone, and when he returned from the war, in 1784, he shed his ministerial standing quickly to go into partnership with Elisha Babcock in a publishing venture, beginning the newspaper *The American Mercury*.

Throughout this period, Barlow's intellectual life concentrated on poetry, particularly his epic poem *The Vision of Columbus*. He did not complete and publish the work until 1787, although he had written the bulk of it by 1783.[17] The poem, modeled to some extent on Milton's *Paradise Lost*, presents Christopher Columbus receiving an angel while he languishes in prison. The angel shows Columbus a vision of the progress of the Western Hemisphere since his landing there. Barlow writes of the native civilizations of both North and South America, of the French and Indian War and the American revolution and their heroes, of the progress of science, art, and literature,[18] and concludes with a vision of a world whose leaders have come together in peace in a "general council of all nations." Barlow also devotes numerous verses to expounding the philosophy which will result in this peaceful world.

Here all religion rests, and soon thy race
Her purest lights, by wisdom's eye shall trace.

---

15. Cited in Zunder, 100.

16. Woodress, *Yankee's Odyssey*, 56.

17. Leon Howard, *The Connecticut Wits*, 159.

18. This section includes verses on Barlow's contemporaries including Trumbull and Dwight. Of Dwight he writes: "For daring Dwight the Epic Muse sublime/Hails her new empire on the western clime./Fired with the themes by seers seraphic sung,/Heaven in his eye, and rapture on his tongue/His voice divine revives the promised land,/The heaven-taught Leader and the chosen band." Cited in Zunder, *Early Days*, 214.

Here the last flights of science shall ascend,
To look thro' heaven, and sense with reason blend
View the great source of love, that flows abroad,
Spreads to all creatures, centres still in God,
Lives thro' the whole, from nature's compact springs,
Orders, reverses, fills the sum of things;
In law constrains, in gospel reconciles,
In judgement frowns, in gentle mercy reconciles,
Commands all sense to feel, all life to prove
The attracting force of universal love.[19]

Barlow's philosophy, a mix of Puritan millennialism and deist idealism, appears in the version of Psalm 140 written shortly after this poem, albeit in more Biblical language:

Let falsehood flee before thy face,
Thy heavenly truth extend,
All nations taste thy heavenly grace,
And all delusion end.

Twentieth-century critics generally conclude that *The Vision of Columbus* "is neither great nor good."[20] In his time, however, Barlow's poem sold well, certainly better than Dwight's counterpart *The Conquest of Canaan*.

While Barlow did the final proofreading of his epic poem, he was, undoubtedly, grateful to receive the commission from the General Association of Connecticut to update Watts' Psalter, a task which ultimately provided him significant income. In 1785, then, the short-lived partnership of Barlow and Babcock produced *Doctor Watts's Imitation of the Psalms of David, corrected and enlarged. By Joel Barlow. To which is added A Collection of Hymns; the Whole applied to the State of the Christian Church in General.* Barlow's preface to the work begins by greatly praising Watts' brilliance as a poet, and then he gives his rationale—and presumably that of the General Association of Connecticut—for this revision:

Were it not for his local appropriation of some Psalms, and his omission of a few others, his Version would doubtless have been used for many ages without an amendment. But as the author of these corrections is employed, directed and supported by so respectable a Body as the whole Clergy of the State; and as it is an object of great importance that harmony and uniformity should be established as extensively as possible in the use of Psalmody, he has not only avoided all local

---

19. Zunder, *Early Days*, 216.
20. Zunder, *Early Days*, 218.

applications, but has made some slighter corrections in point of elegance, where the rules of grammar, established since the time of Doctor Watts, have made it necessary.[21]

Barlow also notes that the Psalms that have been "considerably altered" are 21, 66, 67, 75, 124, 147. As will be shown in the next chapter, Barlow is modest in taking credit for these few alterations, as he and his collaborators altered a number of other Psalms as well.

Like Mycall, and unlike Dwight, Barlow did not work alone on his version of the Psalms. Considerable evidence exists that his fellow Connecticut Wits John Trumbull and Dr. Lemuel Hopkins worked with him on the project.[22] Howard comments that

> The exact authorship of the various revisions and even of the completely new versions cannot be determined, but Barlow apparently did the eighty-eighth and the one hundred and thirty-seventh paraphrases and had the general editorial responsibility for the lot.[23]

Vernon Parrington goes so far as to say that Barlow did not even write the version of Psalm 137, but attributes it to Hopkins.[24] An article in the 1843 *Poets and Poetry of America* notes that a "memorandum" was discovered in Trumbull's papers "which settles the question in favour of Barlow."[25]

It certainly is probable that at least Trumbull and Hopkins made some contribution to the text. Few written records remain of Dr.

---

21. *Doctor Watts's Imitation. . . .*, 1785, preface.

22. The Connecticut Wits, sometimes referred to as the Hartford Wits or the Friendly Club, comprised a fluid group of poets and satirists from the 1780s to the turn of the century. Members met to discuss political and literary matters and collaborated on projects. The group included at one time or another Barlow, Dwight, John Trumbull, David Humphreys, Lemuel Hopkins, Theodore Dwight, Richard Alsop, and Elihu Smith, among others.

23. Howard, *Connecticut Wits*, 161. A dissenting note about Barlow's authorship of Psalm 137 appears in a handwritten note on the inside front cover of a copy of Watts' Psalter (title page missing) held at the Beinecke Rare Book and Manuscript Library at Yale University. The book belonged to Hopkins' nephew, who writes "The Psalm *Along the Banks whose Babel current flows* in Barlow's version is wholly by my Uncle. JMH" The back cover notes in the same handwriting "This is the copy used by my uncle Doctor Lemuel Hopkins in the revision of M. Barlow in which he assisted."

24. Vernon Parrington, *The Connecticut Wits* (Hamden, Connecticut: Archon Books, 1926), iv, 420.

25. Rufus Griswold, *The Poets and Poetry of America* (Philadelphia: Carey and Hart, 1843), 24.

Lemuel Hopkins (a few poems collected in nineteenth-century an-
thologies, treatises on tuberculosis and the common cold). Born in
1750, Hopkins began practicing medicine in Litchfield, Connecticut, in 1776.[26] In 1784 he moved to Hartford and stayed for a time
with Joel Barlow while his house was being prepared. The timing
would indicate that Barlow was working on the Psalter while Hopkins lived with him. His extant poetry is political or satirical,
"chiefly remarkable for their sharp, bitter, biting wit, expressed in
their assaults against charlatanism, hypocrisy and infidelism."[27]
Hopkins did write a poem attacking Ethan Allen for his contempt
of the Bible. His main literary fame came in his collaboration first
with Trumbull, Barlow, and Humphries on *The Anarchiad*, a series
of satirical verses published in newspapers promoting a strong federal government. He later collaborated with the second generation
of Connecticut Wits on *The Echo* and *The Political Green House*,
similar sets of satirical verse serialized in newspapers in Connecticut. Hopkins died in 1801.

James Thacher in 1828 expressed the opinion that Hopkins was
responsible for Psalm 88 in Barlow's Watts "which has been much
admired for its spirit and justice to the original."[28] A copy of Watts'
Psalter that belonged at one time to Hopkins' nephew appears to be
the working manuscript of Hopkins' contributions to the Psalter.
Numerous notes appear in the margins, including a cross by every
overtly British reference. Several changes were suggested that did
not ultimately appear in Barlow's version.[29] At several points, Hopkins crosses out entire Psalms, such as 21, and notes in the margin:
"Rewritten," which, indeed, they were. Oddly, though, in light of
Thacher's comment above that Hopkins wrote the 88th, there are
no marks at all on that Psalm in this book. The thorough nature of
Hopkins' notes on this copy of Watts indicates the depth of the
changes the collaborators considered: initially even more changes
than ultimately appeared, most of them for poetic rather than political reasons.

The case for Trumbull's participation in Barlow's Psalter project
is even stronger. Trumbull, the son of a Congregational minister,

---

26. Walter Steiner, M. D., "Dr. Lemuel Hopkins, One of the Celebrated
Hartford Wits, and a Forgotten, Distinguished American Student of Tuberculosis," *Johns Hopkins Hospital Bulletin*, 21 (January 1910): 17.

27. Ibid., 24.

28. James M. Thacher, *American Medical Biography* (Boston, 1828), 303.

29. For example, Hopkins suggested a change in Psalm 3 CM, verse five,
line two from Watts' "In spite of all my foes" to "And mid my secret foes."
Barlow stayed with Watts.

was a poet by profession and a fellow Yale graduate.[30] His Puritan influences included his mother, who was the granddaughter of Solomon Stoddard and the cousin of Jonathan Edwards. Cowie notes the other two most profound influences on his verse were the neoclassicism in vogue among British poets of the time (Pope, Swift, etc.) and the American revolution. In addition, Watts provided young Trumbull's introduction to poetry. "The first poet he read was Isaac Watts . . . . Trumbull memorized Watts's 'Lyrics' " (i.e., *Horae Lyricae*). Trumbull's first poem, at age four, was a hymn:

> Come, Blessed Saviour, quickly come,
> And call a sinner to thine home,
> Where in thy bosom I may dwell,
> And in the ways of grace excell.[31]

This work inspired Trumbull to work on his own versification of the Psalms "half of which he finished before he was nine."[32]

Trumbull spent years at Yale, as an undergraduate, a graduate student, and a tutor, during the time Timothy Dwight attended as a student. Trumbull and Dwight collaborated on trying to introduce more "belles lettres" into the curriculum. Trumbull also discovered his real penchant for satirical or comic verse, despite his desire to write serious, *American* poetry. In 1770, Trumbull wrote *A Prospect of our Future Glory* along the common theme of the rise of America and the coming moral and cultural fall of Britain.[33] Included in the poem are these lines:

> Some future Shakespeare charm the rising age,
> And hold in magic chains the listening stage;
> Another Watts shall string the heavenly lyre,
> And other Muses other bards inspire.[34]

Clearly Trumbull, as Barlow and the other "Wits", desired above all to create a truly American literary corpus, despite the fact that all wrote in imitation, to one degree or another, of British models.

---

30. The definitive biography of Trumbull remains Alexander Cowie, *John Trumbull Connecticut Wit* (Chapel Hill: University of North Carolina Press, 1936).

31. Ibid., 17.

32. Ibid., 23.

33. This was a common theme of American poets of the times, including Dwight and Barlow, and appears in some of the Psalms in both men's Psalters.

34. Ibid., 61.

Trumbull and Barlow certainly would have agreed on ecclesiastical matters. Taking a position somewhere between strict Calvinism and deism (though publically chastizing deists), Trumbull wrote often about hypocrisy and mediocrity among the clergy. His second most famous poem (after the revolutionary War satire *M'Fingal*), *The Progress of Dulness*, tells the story of "Tom Brainless" who goes to Yale and becomes a mediocre preacher foisted upon an unsuspecting church. Trumbull thought deists were less a threat to the church than these dull clergy and their dull worship services.[35] Trumbull also produced two poems that were free paraphrases of scripture (Cowie calls the second an "imitation"): *The Prophecy of Balaam* from Numbers 23–24 and *The Destruction of Babylon* from selected passages in Isaiah and Revelation. Clearly Trumbull's background made him the ideal collaborator for Barlow on this project.[36]

Considerable dissent exists among Barlow's contemporaries and subsequent commentators on exactly what Barlow and his collaborators did to Watts and why. Ezra Stiles records in his Diary for April 18, 1785,

> Mr. Barlow has *corrected* so much as to assume the *Place* of the Author, as if he was the Author. I think he has corrected too much and unecessarily mutilated the Book and sometimes hurt the poetry . . . . for as the matter is now Barlow has mounted up at one Leap to all the Glory of Watts. This is a new way of Elevation of Genius and Acquest of Honor . . . . Mr. Barlow is an excellent Poet; yet he cannot retouch Watts to advantage.[37]

Stiles was particularly irritated that Barlow put his own name on the cover page along with Watts'. Edward Ninde, writing in 1921, echoes Stiles' words in noting that Barlow was popular with Presbyterians, but not Congregationalists, who thought he had "far exceeded his instructions, and instead of simply 'accommodating' certain Psalms, he had made bold to revise Watts wherever it suited his fancy."[38] O.E. Daggett in an 1846 *New Englander* article praises

---

35. Ibid., 105.

36. A more detailed literary analysis of the poetry of Trumbull, Hopkins, and Barlow would yield more data on exactly who wrote which paraphrases and new additions. That analysis is beyond the scope of this project. This author assumes that Barlow as editor was the final arbiter of the Psalter's contents and may even have altered his collaborators' contributions, so the Psalter will be referred to as Barlow's Watts.

37. Stiles, *Literary Diary*, III, 156.

38. Edward Ninde, *The Story of the American Hymn* (New York: Abingdon, 1921), 33.

Barlow's revisions as showing "at least a respectable skill in composition" but then goes on to add

> he seems to have gone beyond the design of his employers, making so
> many verbal changes which were needless or trivial, and sometimes
> worse, that his readers must have been offended by the violence done
> to their sacred associations.[39]

In a similar vein, a story is told of Barlow encountering a local Hartford street poet named Arnold in a bookstore one day. One of Barlow's contemporaries claims that Arnold addressed to Barlow the following verse:

> Tis God's blest praise you've sought to alter,
> And for your pains deserve a halter;
> You've proved yourself a simple creature,
> Murder'd great Watts, and ruin'd metre.[40]

On the other hand, Barlow's version draws praise from a variety of quarters. The anonymous writer of an 1873 article on Barlow for *The New Englander* remembers the reception of the book differently:

> Barlow . . . accomplished the work committed to him, to their [the
> General Association's] satisfaction, and in some particulars far ex-
> ceeded their expectations. The alterations he made in Watts were, in
> the main, judicious and happy.[41]

This author and others single out Barlow's addition of a version of Psalm 137 ("Along the banks where Babel's current flows") as one of the finest poems of the age. In fact, the author compares it to the better-known Dwight version of that Psalm ("I love thy kingdom, Lord"), noting that Dwight takes too many liberties with the text and Barlow's is truly more of a Psalm paraphrase—an ironic point considering the subsequent relationship between Dwight and Barlow's versions of the *Psalms*.

Despite the reactions of Stiles and more modern commentators, Barlow's version was fairly well received. Barlow received a letter from a contemporary, Joseph Huntington of Coventry, which included the following testimonial:

---

39. O. E. Daggett, "The Psalms in Worship," *The New Englander*, July 1846: 327.

40. Cited in Zunder, *Early Days*, 173.

41. *The New Englander*, 124 (July 1873): 416.

Your emendations of this excellent work are such, Sir, that I trust no more copies will ever be printed without them; and I am very sure no persons of taste and judgment will ever purchase any of the former copies if they can be well supplied with yours. The introduction of your work in congregations may be somewhat gradual, for reasons as well in your view as mine; but it will in due time become universal . . . .[42]

This letter hints at the fact that liturgical change is slow, liturgy by nature being conservative, especially in a culture that memorized the Psalms used in worship and private devotion. Howard presents perhaps the most balanced view of the reception of the book:

The revisions were perhaps excessive, but the whole received general approval and praise except for the natural objections to a change from habitual usage—and some of these may have been unjust metrical criticisms resulting from the fact that Barlow was sympathetic enough with Webster's theories of pronounciation to spell out a few of the words Watts habitually abbreviated.[43]

Not only did the political changes necessitate new imitations of the Psalms, but the language itself was changing. Barlow's close association at Yale with Noah Webster provided a strong motivation to stay on the leading edge of those changes. As Barlow's later life would prove, "he was as receptive to new ideas as Timothy Dwight was impervious."[44]

If subsequent printing history is a gauge of success, Barlow's book made a tremendous impact. The listing in appendix one makes clear that Barlow's version had an extensive printing history in New England, and chapter five notes the adaptations of Barlow's work by other compilers. The Presbyterians in the Middle Atlantic region adopted Barlow wholeheartedly, with numerous editions published well into the 1830s. Even in Barlow's time, Isaiah Thomas freely adapted Barlow's revisions in 1786 and subsequently printed at least three more editions of this adaptation.[45] Barlow also published a separate edition consisting solely of the Psalms and hymns he himself (and Trumbull and Hopkins?) added to Watts. He then extricated himself from the publishing business altogether and opened a store. "The edition of *Watts' Psalms* sold briskly, probably better than the rum, sugar, molasses, tea and other items . . . so that he was

---

42. Zunder, *Early Days*, 184.
43. Howard, *Connecticut Wits*, 161.
44. Parrington, *The Connecticut Wits*, xliv.
45. Benson, "The American Revisions," 25–33.

able to pay his bills and read law."[46] Without question, Barlow's versions of the Psalms held an influence far beyond Connecticut and the Congregational churches there, an influence that has largely been ignored or forgotten.

While Todd claims that "Barlow's version was well received by the New England churches, and was in constant use among them until rumors of the poet's lapse from orthodoxy became . . . rife,"[47] Benson asserts that Barlow's version never really spread beyond the Connecticut churches. He also notes that no new editions seem to have appeared in New England after 1791, suggesting that the use of the Psalter ceased around that time.[48] Of course, Benson's information was limited, and current records make clear Barlow's continuing use.[49] One might also challenge Benson's assumptions by noting that lack of continued printing does not mean an immediate stop in usage. Churches and individuals who bought the Barlow Watts or the Worcester adaptation of it in 1791 or 1795 are unlikely, on a practical basis, to have bought new books for use in worship and devotion the next year. The local church records noted in chapter five reveal that churches were slow to change Psalters or anything else about worship.

While running his store and supervising sales of the Psalter, Barlow read law and was admitted to the Connecticut bar in 1786. His examination paper reveals the continuation of Barlow's progression away from Calvinistic orthodoxy. He argues that laws of nature and society are inseparable and God-given. "Thus if nature and man are governed by laws emanating from the same source, there must be divine sanction for social and legal change."[50] As the previous chapter noted, the multitude of changes in American society in the last half of the eighteenth century consumed more than one church—and secular—leader. Barlow saw the changes as having a divine source and sanction, and he acted on that belief. Ultimately the "respectable Body" of the Congregational clergy of Connecticut understood matters differently, and that difference of opinion affected the use of Watts, and Barlow's Watts in particular, among the Congregational churches.

Barlow continued to move with the changes all around him. He entered into a partnership in land speculation in Ohio, which ultimately sent him on his first journey abroad, to France and England,

46. Woodress, *Yankee's Odyssey*, 80.
47. Todd, *Life and Letters*, 49.
48. Benson, "The American Revisions," 81.
49. Ibid., 32-33.
50. Cited in Woodress, *Yankee's Odyssey*, 81.

and the beginning of the downfall of his reputation among the Connecticut divines. While abroad in the 1790s, Barlow became associated with deism and atheism. He met regularly in London with William Godwin, Mary Wollstonecraft, and others whose names were often linked with "radical" ideas.[51] Barlow translated into English Volney's *Les Ruines*,

> an over-simplified study of comparative religion explaining the common origin of all religious ideas. All established religions are alike in that they are the means of tyranny and oppression, by which unscrupulous and designing men obtain power and wealth by priestcraft.[52]

The work was popularly linked with Paine's *Age of Reason*, and Paine and Ethan Allen were regularly castigated by Congregational leaders as atheists. Probably the final straw for the Connecticut clergy power structure was Barlow's close association with Thomas Jefferson (he eventually became Jefferson's envoy to Napoleon), the proponent of disestablishment himself.

Considerable historical debate exists on how far Barlow strayed from the Calvinism of Yale and his youth. Despite his brief stint in the clergy, Barlow clearly never felt any deep attachment to the church. Indeed, May observes that "like Jefferson . . . Barlow usually claimed in public that he opposed only the historical trappings of Christianity and not its true spirit."[53] His subsequent writings continue to express millennial thoughts about America as a light to the nations, but the religious tone of those thoughts changes. For example, late in life, Barlow made a major revision of *The Vision of Columbus*, and removed from it any theological referents, replacing them with classical figures and renaming the work *The Columbiad*.[54] In addition he wrote a most revealing letter to his wife from Algiers in 1796 in which he describes the punishments meted out by Muslim rulers to "infidels" who entered mosques. Barlow notes that one had to either convert to Islam, or, if a Jew, be burned alive. Christians were hanged for the same offense. He responded to this law with these thoughts: "If it happens to me through intoxication or some other accident to fall into this death, I shall become a Mohammedan immediately, for I have not enough religion of any kind

---

51. Henry F. May, *The Enlightenment in America* (New York: Oxford University Press, 1976), 239.

52. Adolf Koch, *Religion and the American Enlightenment* (New York: Thomas Crowell, 1933), 72.

53. May, *Enlightenment*, 241.

54. Howard, 312–13.

to make me a martyr."[55] Whatever the truth of the matter, Barlow
defended his Christianity on his trips home, being especially
wounded by his old friend Noah Webster's condemnation of his
infidelity.[56]

Most commentators agree that Barlow's declining reputation
spurred the General Association of Connecticut into seeking another revision to replace Barlow's Watts. Though Stiles and others
complained of the quality and quantity of revisions, this problem
did not seem egregious enough to stop the use of the book. No call
for another version came until 1797.

Benson disputes this reasoning, claiming that the advertisement
for Dwight's Watts makes it clear that the true reason for yet another revision was to eliminate Barlow's superfluous changes. He
quotes this advertisement in which Dwight explains he was "cau-
tioned to make no alterations, except those, which should appear to
be either absolutely necessary or plainly important," and then goes
on to say "This apologetic tone reflects a public demand for the
restoration of Watts's own text, and the instructions to the reviser
here alluded to show a purpose corresponding to the demand."[57]
Benson offers no other proof for such a "public demand," and Barlow's biographers and other writers generally conclude that the "excessive" revisions had less to do with the call for a replacement for
Barlow's Watts than the change in Barlow's reputation and the response of the powers of the Connecticut churches to that, and perhaps to the changes of the times in general. Moses Tyler sums up
these opinions by writing

> The book had given universal satisfaction, until poor Joel went over to
> France, and dabbled in the French Revolution, and fell, as was sup-
> posed, into all manner of French impiety and abomination. Of course,
> the saints of Connecticut could not be expected to enjoy any longer
> the psalms and hymns of the great sinner of Paris; and the task of
> President Dwight . . . was really to demephitise and disinfect the book;
> it was to cast out of it all the writings of Joel, and to put into it, in
> their stead, as many as possible of the writings of Timothy.[58]

55. Cited in Todd, *Life and Letters*, 127.

56. Woodress, *Yankee's Odyssey*, 169. Webster refused to review *The Columbiad* because of what he saw as "atheistical" tendencies in it.

57. Benson, "The American Revisions," 81–82.

58. Moses Tyler, *Three Men of Letters* (New York: G.P. Putnam's Sons,
1895), 98 n5; see also Daggett, 327; Anonymous in *The New Englander*,
1873, 419. For an opinion concurring with Benson, see Howard, *Connecticut Wits*, 355.

More accurately, Tyler might have said, to put *back* into it as many as possible of the writings of the now-sainted Watts with minimal additions by Dwight.

Timothy Dwight

As noted above, Dwight and Barlow had at one time been close colleagues. Barlow and Dwight worked on poetry together, and their enduring friendship is shown by Ruth Barlow's stay at Greenfield Hill with Dwight and his wife during Joel's trip to London and France in the early 1790s.[59] As Barlow's political and religious views strayed farther and farther from the Connecticut Standing Order, however, the animosity between the two men grew fierce. Writing of the four men most often associated with the Connecticut Wits (Barlow, Dwight, Trumbull, and Humphreys), Howard comments: ". . . no other four men so perfectly reflected the change from a colony to a nation by taking their departure from such a common point and reaching such different ends."[60] As Barlow traveled and wrote poetry, political satire, and reflections on the French revolution, he and Dwight followed vastly different and conflicting paths. Dwight's opinion of Barlow as an atheist and Jeffersonian grew so acrid that upon assuming the presidency of Yale, he immediately ordered that Barlow's portrait be removed from the school.[61] Shortly after Dwight became president, and chemistry was added to Yale's curriculum, Barlow revealed his knowledge of the divide between the two men. He declared that he was delighted with the new curriculum, and that "he would have sent out a chemical apparatus and preparations had he not supposed that, coming from him, the college authorities would make a bonfire of them in the college yard."[62]

Barlow worked on political philosophy in France while Dwight wrote pastoral epics in Greenfield Hill, Connecticut, and assumed the presidency of a school he would re-create as the bastion of Congregational orthodoxy: Yale. "The vehemence of their opposition was more than anything else a product of the difference in the imaginative qualities of two men who were profoundly affected by the

---

59. Todd, *Life and Letters*, 91.

60. Howard, *Connecticut Wits*, 4.

61. Kenneth Silverman, *Timothy Dwight* (New York: Twayne, 1969), 97.

62. Richard Purcell, *Connecticut in Transition 1775–1818* (Washington: American Historical Society, 1918), 27.

events of the age in which they lived."[63] The extreme differences in their imaginative reactions are decidedly reflected in their versions of Watts' *Psalms*.

As Howard notes above, Dwight, like his Connecticut Wit colleagues Barlow, Humphreys, and Trumbull, grew up amid the shifting sands of late colonial America. Born two years before Barlow in 1752, to the third daughter of Jonathan Edwards, Dwight was led from an early age toward Yale and the ministry.[64] Dwight's father was a merchant and Yale graduate who later became a colonial judge. After a precocious childhood (stories abound of Dwight reading Latin by age six under his mother's tutelage[65]), Dwight entered Yale in 1765. He stayed through a time of curricular ferment and leadership changes to graduation in 1769 and two more years of master's study while teaching school in New Haven. In 1771 he was honored by being named a tutor and stayed on in that capacity another six years.[66]

While at Yale, like Barlow, Dwight pressed the faculty to expand the curriculum to include the study of European literature and began work on his version of the great American epic: *The Conquest of Canaan*. Enamored of Pope and Milton, Dwight often wrote in imitation of them.[67] In so doing, he was certainly following in the methodological footsteps of Watts and many others of his age.

Imitation was a literary genre popular in intellectual circles. Watts did for the Hebrew Psalmists what Pope had done for Horace, and what Johnson was shortly to do for Juvenal.[68]

Dwight also became interested in music, which "led him to collect sacred songs and to write a 'Song' ('Look, lovely maid, on yonder flow'r') modeled on Herrick, an interest he later elaborated in his edition of Watts's Psalms."[69] Dwight followed two conven-

---

63. Howard, *Connecticut Wits*, 347.

64. Biographical works on Dwight consulted for this study include Charles Cuningham, *Timothy Dwight 1752–1817* (New York: Macmillan, 1942); Kenneth Silverman, *Timothy Dwight* (New York: Twayne, 1969); Anabelle Wenzke, *Timothy Dwight (1752–1817)* (Lewiston, New York: Edwin Mellen, 1989); and works on the Connecticut Wits.

65. Cuningham, *Dwight 1752–1817*, 1.

66. Ibid., 23.

67. See, for example, his poem "America" written in imitation of Pope's "Messiah," applying Pope's view of England to America. Silverman, *Timothy Dwight*, 22.

68. Harry Escott, *Isaac Watts Hymnographer* (London: Independent Press, 1962), 169.

69. Ibid., 21.

tions common among American poets of the time still searching for an American voice: imitation of European poets and the wide use of allegory, especially in regard to Biblical and Classical images.[70]

Dwight also wrote with the Puritan heritage strongly in mind. His 1776 Valedictory Address at Yale overflows with millennial imagery. Stephen Berk notes this address shows Dwight's concept of America as an

> empire [that] was to unify many nations under a single political and religious system. While Dwight envisioned a vast realm of freedom and enlightenment, his conception of liberty and knowledge was akin to the Puritan ideal that each individual be free to receive instruction in a single set of beliefs.[71]

In October 1777, the war finally called to Dwight as it had to so many other Yale students and faculty, and he joined Parson's brigade as a chaplain. During his time in the military, he wrote his epic in earnest, as Barlow had his, and Dwight wrote to General Washington to ask if the poem might be dedicated to him. Washington was delighted and when the poem was finally published, in 1785 (by Elisha Babcock), the dedication held.[72]

During the war, Dwight's family found itself in a bit of a scandal. Dwight's father, as a judge, felt he could not break the vow he made to serve the King, yet he had sympathies with the revolution. His solution to the problem was to enter into a land deal with his in-laws in Natchez, Mississippi, to which he traveled with his sister and two of his sons. Unfortunately travel and disease took their toll, and Dwight's father died some months later. His sons returned with nothing to show for their venture but the suspicion of the townspeople that the Dwights were loyalists.[73]

In 1778, therefore, Timothy Dwight returned home to Northampton, Massachusetts, to run his mother's farm and support his siblings, his wife, and his young son. Dwight also founded a coeducational school, which created further controversy. Dwight firmly believed in the importance of educating girls on an equal basis with boys, and both the Northampton and the later school he ran in

---

70. See, for example, his Dec. 18, 1777 "A Sermon, preached at Stamford . . . upon the General Thanksgiving," in which he compares the revolution to the war between Judea and Assyria.

71. Stephen Berk, *Calvinism versus Democracy: Timothy Dwight and the Origins of American Evangelical Orthodoxy* (Hamden, Connecticut: Archon Books, 1974), 22.

72. Silverman, *Timothy Dwight*, 24.

73. Cuningham, *Dwight 1752–1817*, 88ff.

Greenfield Hill admitted both sexes. His school ultimately became so popular that Ezra Stiles is said to have felt it as competition with Yale.[74]

Finally, in May 1783, with his family back on its feet and the war over, Dwight received and accepted a call to be pastor at Greenfield Hill, Connecticut, overlooking Long Island Sound. His most prolific writing phase of his life began here, as did his most politically and theologically conservative period. He became, once again, a schoolmaster, running an Academy that was so popular that "a thousand pupils, from every part of the United States, resorted to it within the next twelve years."[75]

In addition to his sermons and articles, three major poems illustrate Dwight's political, social, and religious ideas in the years after the revolution. *The Conquest of Canaan* (1785), *The Triumph of Infidelity* (1788) and *Greenfield Hill* (1794) show Dwight's progress from a man immersed in a revolution to one who feared new social, political, and religious ideas. He favored a parochialism that saw rural Connecticut and modified Puritan values as the place and mode of millennial fulfillment. Instead of simply understanding America as the new Israel, Dwight increasingly came to see the Church in America (or specifically the Congregational Church in Connecticut) as the instrument to save the United States for its role as beacon to the world.

The Conquest of Canaan, written in imitation of Milton, allegedly tells the story of Joshua and various Biblical and original characters moving into the Promised Land.[76] Despite the widespread use of allegory among American poets of the time, including the other Connecticut Wits, Dwight insisted the poem was not about the American revolution. Oddly enough, the poem does contain "apostrophes," which exalt the revolutionary exploits of Nathan Hale and other American heroes. Silverman and twentieth-century literary critics, as well as Dwight's contemporaries, however, read the poem as intentionally allegorical. "To fully understand his [Dwight's] writings one must translate the broken cisterns into Jefferson or Sharp, the rising empires into Washington or Eli Whitney."[77]

74. Ibid., 94–95.

75. Edwin F. Hatfield, *The Poets of the Church* (Boston: Milford House, 1884), 218. Hatfield also includes a brief biographical sketch of Barlow, therefore definitely considering him a "poet of the church," despite his subsequent reputation.

76. Timothy Dwight, "The Conquest of Canaan," in *The Major Poems of Timothy Dwight*, William McTaggart and William Bottorff, eds. (Gainesville, Fla: Scholars' Facsimiles and Reprints, 1969).

77. Silverman, *Timothy Dwight*, Preface.

Dwight's dedication of the poem to George Washington would seem to make his intentions clear.

The poem's reception indicates that perhaps his method proved too subtle for many readers. Sales were few and the poem was largely ignored in America. "Unfortunately for Dwight, his epic appeared at the same time as Barlow's more clearly topical *Vision of Columbus*, with which it was often unfavorably compared, no doubt feeding Dwight's growing hatred of Barlow."[78]

Part of the problem for Dwight and the other budding American poets concerned the search for a language, a true American poetic idiom, in which to write. Barlow expressed this struggle in a Fourth of July speech, noting that "the 'practical tone and tension' of the American mind is incongruent with its abstract principles: 'We are like a person conversing in a foreign language, whose idiom is not yet familiar to him.' "[79] Much later in his career, Dwight wrote *Observations on Language* (1806) in which he explains that "language reflects national character, since *'nations will uniformly have such worlds as express those ideas which they wish to communicate.'* "[80]

Dwight continued to struggle to communicate the ideas he thought formed the "world" of America and his vision of religion's place in it. He saw no division between the two concepts, and the move toward disestablishment—and the rising vogue to imitate things European (particularly French and British)—confounded him. He responded to this perceived discontinuity in American ideas and practice with the anonymously published *The Triumph of Infidelity* (1788).[81] Satan narrates the poem, telling of the victory of his servants Hume, Voltaire, and others and lifting up deism and universalism as Satan's tools to destroy the millennial promise of America. In case this poem was felt too subtle, Dwight, writing as "Scriblerus," provided footnotes to explain obscure sections. The poem is angry and sharp, and reaction to it reflected its tone—and public opinion concerning Dwight. "The poem is a last-ditch effort, through poetry, to combat what he saw as a waning orthodoxy among Americans of his time and place."[82] Silverman continues that ". . . the poem attacks not only skeptics or liberal Calvinists, but all the forces of social instability."[83] For Dwight, the social changes

---

78. Ibid., 42.

79. Cited in Silverman, *Timothy Dwight*, 60.

80. Timothy Dwight, *Observations on Language*, in *Memoirs of the Connecticut Academy of Arts and Sciences*, Vol. I (New Haven: Oliver Steele, 1806), 365.

81. McTaggart and Bottorff, eds., *Major Poems*, 327–66.

82. Ibid., xiv.

83. Silverman, *Timothy Dwight*, 87.

brought about after the revolution, the threats (real or perceived) from France (including the Illuminati controversy), and the rise in theological challenges to the Standing Order in New England all threatened the possibility of America becoming the "light to the nations" he envisioned during the revolutionary era, and that his Puritan ancestors had seen from the beginning. For Dwight, more was at stake than just the future of the Congregational churches.

As Barlow became more cosmopolitan, both in ideas and lifestyle, Dwight became more parochial. "The zenith of Dwight's parochialism was his millennial belief that Connecticut's institutions would eventually revivify the world."[84] His last important poetic effort, *Greenfield Hill* (1794),[85] clearly reflects this turn in Dwight's social and theological thought. This pastoral epic enshrines the village life of rural Connecticut, no longer America as a whole or even New England, as the ideal setting for living out the Kingdom of God on Earth. He modeled each section of the poem after a different English poet, and he seemed to assert that rural Connecticut was "sort of a purged Europe, where for the first time poetic conventions became realities."[86] The fifth section of the poem consists of a dying clergyman's last advice to his parishioners. He spends considerable time telling them how fleeting life is and how they must seize every chance to obey God and live aright (echoes of Jonathan Edwards, perhaps?), and then gives advice on how to arrange everyday affairs. He includes instruction on daily religious devotion, hard work, care for the poor and ill, and observing the Sabbath. Section six continues the advice, with the advisor being an old farmer, whose major child-rearing counsel, italicized so as not to be missed, is:

> Habits alone through life endure,
> Habits alone your child secure.

The habits concern what the clergyman had already laid forth: hard work, attention to worship and devotion, care for family and the needy.

This poem, perhaps more than Dwight's sermons or theological writings, makes clear the pragmatic approach Dwight took toward happiness and obedience to God, as well as his theological understanding of America's place in God's realm. Hathaway reads Dwight with this understanding:

> In Dwight's millennial vision . . . progress was defined as stability, the retention and spread, throughout the nation, of the blessings of mod-

---

84. Berk, *Calvinism*, 42.
85. McTaggart and Bottorff, eds., *Major Poems*, 367–542.
86. Silverman, *Timothy Dwight*, 59.

est competence and orthodoxy .... Timothy Dwight was saying that America's gift to the future was not restless change, for the sake of change, not mere revolution, but the possibility of stabilizing the ideal present, universalizing it in time and space.[87]

Berk calls Dwight's approach "supernatural rationalism," which Berk feels "humanizes" his orthodoxy. He sought to "simplify theology so that the average person could grasp its meaning."

> Throughout his theology, he carefully grounded each doctrine in the circumstances of life. His system was not one of abstract reasoning conceived in isolation from the daily currents of existence .... Dwight's goal was to make orthodoxy an appealing system by proving it most useful in giving man (sic) happiness. He sought to harmonize Calvinism with the humanistic and utilitarian values of middle class America.[88]

For Dwight, the parish of Greenfield Hill epitomized these values and gave his theology—and his poetry—flesh.

Dwight's understanding of scripture melds with this desire for simple and plain meaning in theology. From the time he was a student at Yale (and his 1772 "Dissertation on the History, Eloquence and Poetry of the Bible"), to his later series of sermons as Yale president which allegedly led to the Second Great Awakening there, Dwight saw the Bible as a literary work with a clear meaning. "In an age still overfond of debating abstractions, Dwight dared to proclaim the plain meaning of the Bible to be the true meaning."[89] His Puritan ancestors had stressed relevance in prayer and preaching, and thus in the use of the Bible. For Dwight, this translated to an emphasis on "particulars over generalities,"[90] his hermeneutic stressing the specificity of the Bible. Certainly his poetry reflects that, choosing sometimes references to obscure stories over general principles. Thus he felt that each person could find in the scripture wisdom suited to their particular place in life. Sometimes that might require stretching the text, as Dwight interprets rather liberally the Biblical story and personalities in *The Conquest of Canaan*, transposing time sequences and inventing new characters. Clearly his poetry is "imitation" of scripture rather than translation or even paraphrase.

---

87. Richard Hathaway, *Sylvester Judd's New England* (University Park: Penn State University Press, 1981), 58–59.

88. Berk, *Calvinism*, 80, 82, 100.

89. Cuningham, *Dwight 1752–1817*, 319.

90. Silverman, *Timothy Dwight*, 26–27.

At least in poetic conventions, he shared Watts' hermeneutic. The important goal was to get the meaning across to the reader, and both the Bible and good poetry might suffer in the process. Vernon Parrington comments "that he could ever have been looked upon as a great poet is a fact to be wondered at."[91]

As the century came to a close, and as he left Greenfield Hill in 1795 to become President of Yale, Dwight became more and more concerned about the growth of infidelity and moral degeneration he perceived among the American people. He began to write and preach at length on the subject, and his writings stress the importance of public worship to change this state of affairs. In his *Travels in New England and New York*, written over a period of more than twenty years and published posthumously, he observes

> But religion cannot exist, and has never existed, for any length of time, without public worship . . . . where there is no religion, there is no morality. Moral obligation has its sole ground in the character and government of God. But where God is not worshipped, his character will soon be disregarded . . . . Justice, kindness, and truth, the great hinges on which free society hangs, will be unpracticed, because there will be no motives to the practice, or sufficient forces to resist the passions of men.[92]

The lack of student membership and participation in the college chapel at Yale prompted Dwight to call for a revival there. His concern about worship even entered into his discussion of the French revolution in his 1798 "The Duty of Americans at the Present Crisis":

> For what end shall we be connected with men of whom this [infidelity] is the character and conduct? . . . . Is it that our churches may become temples of reason, our Sabbath a decade, and our Psalms of praise Marsellois (sic) hymns?[93]

Finally, Dwight's criticism of the new United States Constitution contains a concern about worship. In "The True Means of Establishing Public Happiness" (1795), Dwight notes that events like the Whiskey Rebellion prove that "freedom is not enough: men can be free and miserable. The aim of life, rather, is happiness, which de-

---

91. Parrington, *The Connecticut Wits*, xlii.

92. Cited in Robert T. Handy, *A Christian America* (New York: Oxford University Press, 1984), 21.

93. Cited in Charles Roy Keller, *The Second Great Awakening in Connecticut* (New Haven: Yale University Press, 1942), 19–20.

pends on virtue, which depends on 'Religious Education and Public Worship' which the Constitution ignored."[94]

This regard for public worship drew Dwight not only to revitalize worship at Yale's Chapel, but to a project of the General Association of Connecticut to make yet another revision of Watts' *Psalms of David Imitated.* As noted above, the Connecticut clergy saw a need to replace Barlow's revision either because of its "unnecessary changes" or due to Barlow's declining reputation among Connecticut's Congregational establishment. The minutes of the meeting commissioning Dwight to provide a new version shed little light on the matter:

> Mr. Mansfield, Mr. Mills, Dr. Edwards [Jonathan Edwards' son] and Mr. E. Atwater were appointed to bring in a report concerning Mr. Barlow's alteration of Dr. Watts' Psalms; and they exhibited the following: Whereas in some of Dr. Watts's translation of the Psalms, there are expressions confined to particular places or countries; and whereas Dr. Watts did not translate some of David's Psalms, therefore resolved by this General Association, that application be made to President Dwight, that he would alter those passages which are confined as aforesaid: and translate those Psalms which Dr. Watts did not translate; and that a committee of this body be appointed to review, both the alteration and the translations, which President Dwight shall make, and to correct or approve the same.[95]

Note that this time the members of the Association were taking no chances. They appointed a review committee and specifically instructed Dwight only to revise those Psalms with particularly offensive referents and translate what Watts left out. As chapter five will explore, Dwight followed their instructions quite closely, with few changes other than those related to British references. His own explanation of the project, written in the "Advertisement" in the front of the book, states

> In making such alterations in Doctor Watts's version as respected objects merely local, I have in some instances applied the Psalm or the passage, to the Church at large, or to Christian nations generally; and in others, particularly to our own country. The latter I have done because every nation, like every individual, feeling its own concerns more than any other, will find various occasions of adapting its praise peculiarly to them.[96]

94. Cited in Silverman, *Timothy Dwight*, 95.

95. *The Records of the General Association of the Colony of Connecticut June 1738–June 1799* (Hartford: Case, Lockwood and Brainard, 1888), 172.

96. Dwight, *The Psalms of David Imitated . . .*, 1801.

Those "occasions," as indicated above, Dwight felt should occur frequently in the life of the new nation, and should be government-sponsored. At about the time of the publication of Dwight's revision, Dwight participated in the founding of a publication called the *Palladium*, "dedicated to defending clerical influence in politics." His writings there advocate government-supported public worship, because it "benefits even the farmer by teaching large groups of people—more effectively than coercive laws and without expense—decent manners, orderly business tactics, and friendliness."[97] In the series of sermons that allegedly led to the Awakening at Yale, he asserted that "Public prayer, above all things, preserves alive a sense of National dependence on God."[98] Dwight would not do away with all specific national references, for the fate of the nation and the church at prayer were irrevocably intertwined in his understanding of God's plan for America.

Benson observes that Dwight's Psalter also reveals the deep animosity of both Dwight and the Connecticut divines toward Joel Barlow. "Very significant is the fact that everything of his [Barlow's] is eliminated from Dr. Dwight's version."[99] This is not technically true, for Dwight, as a poet, could not miss the fact that some of the things Barlow changed needed to be changed. There are several Psalms in which no particular British reference occurs and yet Dwight changes language, often following the fact that Barlow changed the same line. Dwight's changes are usually different, but they are changes nonetheless.[100]

As the Second Great Awakening dawned, "Dwight's Watts" was published. At least in Connecticut, its reception was highly favorable. So indicates the report of Daggett 45 years later, who notes that Dwight's version has been "used and approved so many years by the Congregational churches in Connecticut (perhaps without an exception), and by many Presbyterian churches in other states."[101] Daggett's 1846 article (and Benson after him) does note that Barlow's version found its way into many other arenas. He mentions

---

97. Silverman, *Timothy Dwight*, 103, 105.

98. Cited in Berk, *Calvinism*, 103.

99. Benson, "The American Revisions . . . ," 83.

100. See, for example, the changes in Psalm 46, First Part, verse 5, line 2 or Psalm 58, verse 1, line 3. There does appear to be at least one place, contrary to Benson, where Dwight accepts a Barlow change: in Psalm 72, Second Part, CM, verse 6, line 4; see further in chapter five.

101. Daggett, "Psalms in Worship," 328. The question of usage by Presbyterian churches proves difficult to assess and is beyond the scope of this study.

the Worcester Watts, which included many of Barlow's changes, and also observes

> that a Presbyterian Assembly, which has been jealous of New England innovations has yet retained in the last collection of Psalms put forth under its sanction, many or most of Barlow's alterations, which were long since eschewed in the region where they originated.[102]

The Presbyterian versions were largely restricted to the Middle Atlantic states and New York, with little usage in New England.[103] See appendix one for the long printing history of Dwight's Watts throughout New England. As with Joel Barlow, Dwight's material also was extensively borrowed for use in other Psalm collections (see chapter six).

Dwight's version sold well enough to enable Dwight to contribute over a thousand dollars to help establish the Missionary Society of Connecticut.[104] His focus in the new century would be on mission, on continuing his quest to bring America back from "infidelity." As opposed to the other Connecticut Wits, Parrington describes Dwight as one in whom there was

> no sap of originality . . . no creative energy, but instead the sound of voices long silent, the chatter of a theology long since disintegrating, the authority of a hierarchy already falling into decay, the tongue in short of a dead past.[105]

Both in the restoration of the original Watts (including some language already becoming archaic in Dwight's time) and in Dwight's new compositions for the Psalter, does one see a last liturgical defense against the threat of Barlow and the deists on one hand, and of unbridled emotional revivalism on the other? Do these texts reflect the larger religious and social tensions of the times during which they were commissioned and composed? An exploration of the specific texts and their use in New England churches will shed light on these and other issues.

---

102. Ibid., 327, footnote.
103. For more detail on the Presbyterian versions of Barlow, see Benson, "The American Revisions . . .," 76ff.
104. Cuningham, *Dwight 1752–1817*, 335.
105. Parrington, *The Connecticut Wits*, cl.

Chapter Five

In Their Own Words:
Specific Psalms Revised

The commissions to both Barlow and Dwight specified that they were to work primarily on the passages in Watts that contained "local" application,[1] and to add those texts Watts had omitted. Stiles assumed Mycall's reasoning to be similar,[2] yet all three revisers made myriad changes in Watts' original text. Out of 341 total Psalms in Watts,[3] 228 Psalms show alterations or additions in one or all of the subsequent revisions. Only 28 of Watts' original texts, however, contained political content that might offend American worshipers.[4] Barlow admits in his preface that he

> not only avoided all local applications, but . . . made some slighter corrections in point of elegance, where the rules of grammar, established since the time of Doctor Watts, have made it necessary.[5]

Although Barlow made many more changes in Watts than either Dwight or Mycall, both of them also changed non-political language without explanation. Dwight added considerably more new texts than Barlow to Watts' original Psalter.[6]

---

1. See chapter four, notes 9 and 95.

2. Mycall's version has no explanatory preface. Stiles, *Literary Diary*, vol. II, 571.

3. *The Psalms of David Imitated* also contains a small selection of hymns, both in Watts' original and in each of the revisions. This volume concerns only the Psalms.

4. See appendix two.

5. Barlow, *Dr. Watts's Imitation*, 1785.

6. Dwight added 32 new or virtually re-written texts while Barlow added 16. Dwight did note that he intended to add texts to be used with "Proper Meter," in addition to writing versions of the 12 Psalms that Watts had

In this chapter we will examine both the revisions and the new texts primarily with an eye toward how the texts reflect the political, theological, and social situations in which their writers lived. In each section, the revisions will be analyzed first, before we turn our attention to the new texts.[7]

Political Language

Twenty-eight of Watts' Psalms show some of what can be called "political language." In thirteen Psalms this language refers directly to Great Britain.[8] In some cases, however, it appears more subtle, as in a reference to kingship or "isles." Austin Phelps, in *Hymns and Choirs* (1860), in which he discusses the reasons for revising the words to hymns and Psalms, addresses Watts' own notes in the first

---

omitted from his edition. Dwight seems to be using the term "proper" in the sense of the French word "propre," meaning that these Psalms had their own tunes, unique, perhaps, in meter from the more commonly used meters. His Psalms in "Proper Meter" do not all have the same meter.

7. See appendix two for a catalogue of the revisions and appendix three for the new texts. Barlow and Mycall especially made numerous small grammatical revisions which are of minimal importance; primary attention here will be given to the more significant changes. The four central texts examined are:

> Isaac Watts, *The Psalms of David Imitated in the Language of the New Testament and applied to the Christian State and Worship* (Hartford: Patten and Webster, 1780). A hand-written note inside this indicates someone felt this was the version Barlow used to make his revisions. I also consulted a first edition, 1719 London, of the Watts.

> *The Psalms of David Imitated in the Language of the New Testament and applied to the Christian State and Worship by I. Watts, D.D.*, 40th edition corrected and accommodated to the Use of the Church of Christ in America (Newburyport: John Mycall, 1781). I also consulted a 1787 Boston edition of the Mycall revision.

> *Doctor Watts's Imitation of the Psalms of David, corrected and enlarged by Joel Barlow* (Hartford: Barlow and Babcock, 1785). I also consulted an 1814 Philadelphia edition of Barlow.

> *The Psalms of David Imitated in the Language of the New Testament and applied to the Christian Use and Worship by I Watts DD.* A new edition in which the Psalms omitted by Dr. Watts are versified anew in proper meter. By Timothy Dwight DD (Hartford: Hudson and Goodwin, 1801).

8. Psalms 19 SM 1st, 21 CM, 47 CM, 60 CM, 67 CM, 75 LM, 96 as 113, 100 LM, 104, 115 as new 150, 135 CM, 145 LM, 147 LM 2nd.

edition of his Psalter. One of these notes, to Psalm 67, explains Watts' thoughts behind this specific use of language:

> Having translated the Scene of this Psalm to great Britain, I have bor-row'd a devout and poetical Wish for the Happiness of my native Land, from Zech. 2:5, and offered it up in the 2d Stanza.[9]

This is consistent with Watts' hermeneutic referred to in chapter three, and indeed with the Puritan sense that prayer should always be particular and relevant.

That same hermeneutic required Mycall, Barlow, and Dwight to modify Watts' language in these Psalms, yet in most cases, each approached that change with a different agenda. The most profound of these revisions occurs in Psalm 21, which Watts paraphrased as a Psalm to Britain's king, subtitling it "Our King is in the Care of Heaven." The first stanza reads:

1. The King, O Lord, with songs of praise
   Shall in thy strength rejoice;
   And, blest with thy salvation, raise
   To heaven his cheerful voice.

Mycall rewrites the subtitle as "America the Care of Heaven," and the first stanza becomes

1. Our States, O Lord, with songs of praise
   Shall in thy strength rejoice;
   And blest with thy salvation raise
   To heaven their cheerful voice.

This illustrates Mycall's pattern throughout his Psalter of simply changing the references to Great Britain or the king into references to the United States. This is a basic hermeneutical transfer from one referent to another, leaving most of the rest of Watts' language unchanged.

Barlow and Dwight, however, make a more complicated move than Mycall. Both men understood their commission as to remove "local" references and apply the Psalm "to the church at large, or to Christian nations generally; and in [some] particularly to our own country."[10] In the case of this Psalm, both apply it particularly, but

---

9. Cited in Austin Phelps, *Hymns and Choirs* (Andover: Warren Draper, 1860), 179–80.

10. Dwight, 1801, Preface.

not as specifically as Mycall. Barlow's version of 1785, subtitled "National Blessings acknowledged," reads:

> 1. In thee great God, with songs of praise,
>   Our favoured realms rejoice;
>   And blest with thy salvation, raise
>   To heaven their cheerful voice.

Barlow goes on in the Psalm to make a fairly clear reference (at least it should have been clear to people singing this within ten years of the revolution) to the recent war, noting in stanzas three and four:

> 3. In deep distress our injured land
>   Implored thy power to save;
>   For life we prayed; thy bounteous hand
>   The timely blessing gave.
>
> 4. Thy mighty arm, eternal Power,
>   Opposed their deadly aim,
>   In mercy swept them from our shore,
>   And spread their sails with shame.

Watts' original refers in these stanzas to the foes of the king:

> 4. But righteous Lord, his stubborn foes
>   Shall feel thy dreadful hand;
>   Thy vengeful arm shall find out those
>   That hate his mild commands.

Fifteen years later, with the revolution less in the forefront of the American consciousness, Dwight returns to the original theme of Watts' version (and, incidentally, the original Biblical Psalm 21), subtitling his work "Rulers are the care of heaven." Dwight does not completely universalize the Psalm, however, for his first stanza reads (italics added):

> 1. *Our* Rulers, Lord, with songs of praise
>   Shall in thy strength rejoice,
>   And blest with thy salvation, raise
>   To heaven their cheerful voice.

This comes from the same pen that dedicated the epic poem "The Conquest of Canaan" to George Washington in 1785. Barlow's war reference disappears from stanza three, which Dwight makes a fairly simple trope on Watts, changing the singular to plural to represent "Our Rulers" instead of "the king." The fourth stanza, however, makes a significant political statement that echoes throughout Dwight. As opposed to Watts' reference in this stanza to the king's foes, Dwight writes (italics added):

> 4. But, righteous Lord, *thy* stubborn foes
>   Shall quake through all their bands;
>   *Thy* vengeful arm shall find out those,
>   That hate *thy* mild commands.

It is not rulers whose commands are avenged by God, but rather God's commands take precedence. The ambiguity in Dwight's third and fourth stanzas begs the question of whether this Psalm warns rulers in America to pay attention to God first and foremost to be assured blessing in rule. Certainly this subtext agrees with Dwight's views on church-state relations, and his horror at French "infidelity." The point seems to be emphasized as Dwight uses stanzas five and six from Watts unchanged:

> 5. When thou against them dost engage
>   Thy just, but dreadful doom,
>   Shall like a fiery oven's rage,
>   Their hopes and them consume.
>
> 6. Thus Lord, thy wondrous power declare,
>   And thus exalt thy fame;
>   Whilst we glad songs of praise prepare
>   For thy almighty name.

The antecedent for the "them" in stanza five is clearly the "stubborn foes" of stanza four, which can refer certainly to the enemies of the rulers who would also be enemies of God, or to the rulers themselves if they make themselves enemies of God. One wonders how Dwight intended this to be heard during the Jefferson presidency.

The other Psalms with specific references to Britain show less dramatic examples of the concerns of the three revisers. Generally, Mycall's pattern of specific local language continues, as in Psalm 135 CM, stanza eight, which begins in Watts:

> O Britain know the living God.

Mycall sings:

> New England know thy living God.

Barlow and Dwight never make such a local allusion. In that Psalm, Barlow generalizes to:

Ye nations know the living God.

Dwight makes the allusion Biblical:

O Zion, trust the living God.

Both Barlow and Dwight use Zion in place of Britain more than once. Barlow and Dwight in Psalm 115 (as new 150) (which both Watts and Dwight subtitle "A Psalm for the 5th of November," Guy Fawkes' Day) alternate using Zion for Britain. Stanza six, lines one and six, in Watts read:

> 6. O Britain, trust the Lord: thy foes in vain . . .
> And Britain blest the Lord that built the skies.

Mycall simply substitutes "Columbia" in both places with no other changes. Barlow, on the other hand, writes:

> 6. In God we trust; our impious foes in vain . . .
> And Zion bless the God that built the skies.

Dwight makes a slightly different move:

> 6. O Zion! trust the Lord: thy foes in vain, . . .
> And saints adore the God, that built the skies.

A similar pattern appears in Psalm 67 CM, which begins in Watts:

> 1. Shine, mighty God, on Britain shine.

Mycall substitutes "on all the land." Barlow and Dwight create corresponding phrases:

Barlow: "Shine, mighty God, on Sion shine."
Dwight: "Shine on our land, Jehovah, shine."

While at first glance, one might assume that the "Zion" references were merely Biblical allusions, the theology of the American churches from their founding indicates that at the time, "our land" and "Sion" would be understood as synonymous. Barlow's Puritan heritage, reflected to some extent in his earlier poems (see especially "The Prospect of Peace"), and Dwight's considerable theological pedigree would indicate the millennial theology that equated Zion and America. Although by 1801 Dwight was less idealistic on this count than earlier in his life, his later poetry, especially *Greenfield Hill*, continues to show millennial themes in his theological and national understanding. This language had been used in worship in America for over a hundred and fifty years, especially in preaching, and the allusion would undoubtedly not be lost on worshipers, especially those who remembered the Watts versions of these Psalms.

Between Mycall's version and Dwight's, twenty years elapsed. Mycall published before the final treaty ending the revolution was signed, Dwight some years after the signing of the Constitution. The changes in political language between the three revisions clearly reflects the shift in national concern. For example, Psalm 67 CM, stanza four, reads in Watts:

4. Sing to the Lord, ye distant lands
   Sing loud with solemn Voice;
   While British tongues exalt his praise
   And British hearts rejoice.

Mycall, writing when the outcome of the revolution was assured, refers specifically to the American situation and transforms the Psalm into one of national thanksgiving:

4. Sing to the Lord, ye rescu'd States
   Sing loud with solemn voice;
   While thankful tongues exalt his praise
   And grateful hearts rejoice.

Both Barlow and Dwight, in a rare example of unanimity, change the first line back to Watts' version, and do two slight variations on what Mycall wrote.

Even by 1785, Barlow is not as specific as Mycall, though elsewhere he makes subtle specific references. Dwight, by 1801, sees no need whatsoever to refer to what is past. The same dynamic occurs in Psalm 75 LM, which Watts subtitles "Power and Government from God Alone. Applied to the Glorious Revolution by King William, or the Happy Accession of George I to the Throne." Mycall, typically, replaces the second sentence with "Applied to the glorious revolution in America, July 4th 1776," making the Psalm unashamedly a national hymn. Barlow continues that theme, subtitling the text "Praise to God for the return of Peace," still obviously connected to the American revolution. Dwight, however, takes the Psalm in an entirely different direction, changing the meter and calling it "Government from God alone. A Psalm for a General Election."

Stanza six in the Watts, Mycall, and Barlow versions illustrate the movement in this Psalm. Watts has been cataloging a change in royalty, and writes:

> 6. No vain pretence to royal birth,
>   Shall fix a tyrant on the throne;
>   God, the great sovereign of the earth,
>   Will rise and make his justice known.

Mycall not-so-subtly changes the emphasis:

> 6. No vain pretence to royal birth
>   Shall chain us to a tyrant's throne;
>   God, the great sovereign of the earth,
>   Shall crush usurpers with his frown.

His readers would have had no doubt about who the tyrant was or mistake the event referred to that resulted in the "crushing."

Barlow goes even farther in describing the significance of recent events (italics added):

> 6. Let haughty tyrants sink their pride,
>   Nor lift so high their scornful head;
>   But lay their impious thoughts aside,
>   *And own the empire God hath made.*

God has not merely crushed a tyrant and broken the chains of the States; by 1785, God has formed an empire.

By 1801, however, Dwight turned Barlow's celebration of God's power into a warning to *America's* rulers. His version of the Psalm is a prayer to God to make the rulers govern the nation well and justly, and to remind them who ultimately has the power—the same warning Mycall and Barlow pronounce to the British tyrants. Stanza five reads:

> 5. Teach them, that greatness, power and place are thine
>   Gifts from thy hand, bestowed for ends divine:
>   Rulers, thy Stewards, to mankind are given
>   To shower the good and build the cause of heaven;
>   From thee a rich reward the faithful know;
>   The faithless hasten to distinguished woe.

In the context of the Federalist controversy with the Jeffersonians, Dwight's request that God teach rulers that their primary task is to "build the cause of heaven" makes a point in the disestablishment discussion. It also illustrates his penchant to understand the identity of the new Israel not as the United States but as the Church, which must save the country for its role as light to the world.

We must note two other idiosyncrasies of the Psalms revised for specific British language. The first concerns the use of the adjective "Western" in place of "British." Only Dwight uses the word this way, and the allusion seems ambiguous. Does he refer to Europe as part of the West, or only to the western side of the Atlantic? In other poetry (specifically "The Conquest of Canaan") he refers to the East meaning the Orient. Is he deliberately, despite his very public aversion to things British and European, including these lands in "Christian nations generally"? An example of this usage occurs in Psalm 147 LM, second part. Watts begins the Psalm, "O Britain, praise thy mighty God" which Mycall changes to "Columbia . . .," Barlow to "Let Zion . . .," but Dwight to "Bless, O Thou Western World, thy God." He makes a similar move in Psalm 47 CM, stanza six, where Watts' "The British islands are the Lord's" becomes in Dwight "These western climes are all the Lord's." Neither Mycall nor Barlow ever use this language.

The second idiosyncrasy occurs in the rare occasions when Dwight retains an obviously British word or phrase where either Mycall or Barlow or both clearly change it. One example already noted is the subtitle to Psalm 115 (as the new 150) where both Mycall and Barlow drop or change the subtitle indicating the Fifth of November while Dwight preserves it. Oddly enough, in Psalm 124 LM, which has the same subtitle in Watts, Dwight changes it to "A song for public deliverance from great calamities." In the same way, in Psalm 65 LM, first part, Watts refers in stanza two, line four, to "islands of the northern sea."

> 2. All Lands to Thee shall lift their Eyes,
>   And Islands of the Northern Sea.

Barlow, sensing Great Britain as the "islands," changes this to "and every yielding heart obey." Dwight ignores the allusion to Britain and retains the line in Watts' form. It is difficult to imagine an American reference for those islands. It seems especially odd that Dwight did not catch this, for he did change Psalm 97 CM which Watts begins "Ye Islands of the Northern sea." Dwight changes this to "Ye nations round the northern sea." (Barlow universalizes by writing "Let earth, with every isle and sea."). Part of the explanation might come from Dwight's (and the Connecticut Association's) concern to conserve as much of Watts as possible in contrast to Barlow's extensive "tampering."

The other changes in language which could be understood as political are mostly minor and mostly Barlow. Mycall includes one revision, which neither Barlow nor Dwight follow, that seems minor but that, in context, takes on greater significance. In Psalm 94 CM, first part, Watts paraphrases verse one as:

1. O God to whom revenge belongs,
   Proclaim thy wrath aloud;
   Let Sov'reign power redress our wrongs
   Let justice smite the proud.

Mycall simply changes the grammar, so that lines two through four read

1. Proclaims his wrath aloud;
   His Sovereign powers redress our wrongs
   His justice smites the proud.

As the revolution comes to an end, these lines read differently than they might some years later to either Barlow or Dwight.

One of the other more minor changes, in this case done at least once by Barlow and Dwight together, concerns the use of the word "oppressed." Watts writes in Psalm 58 (as the 113th) stanza one, line three, "When th'injured poor before you stands," the "you" referring to "Judges." Barlow changes the line completely to read "When vile oppression wastes the land." This resembles his revision of Psalm 82 LM, stanza two, which reads in Barlow "Why will ye frame oppressive laws?" as opposed to Watts' word "wicked" to describe laws. In Psalm 82, Dwight prefers Watts' wording, but in Psalm 58, he follows Barlow, though restoring the original grammar of Watts: "When the oppressed before you stands." "Oppressed" is a much more politically and emotionally charged word than either "injured" or "wicked." Given the political memories of Great Britain's "oppression" of the colonists, this word surely carried a different meaning when sung in the context of judges or law-givers.

The political overtones of the Psalms Barlow and Dwight add to the collection more commonly reflect events current to their day rather than Revolutionary War material. In these Psalms, Dwight especially makes clear his Federalist and anti-Deist (infidel, illuminati, etc.) sentiments.

Barlow is still close enough in time to the war to make subtle references, but these are rare. One occurs in his version of Psalm 52 LM (one of the Psalms omitted by Watts and Mycall). The Biblical

Psalm's subtitle indicates it as words against the unjust Saul, threatening God's vengeance. The Psalm begins "Why boasteth thou thyself in mischief, O mighty man?"[11] Barlow subtitles the Psalm "The folly of self-dependence." American singers could hardly help but assume that folly belonged to *their* former rulers:

1. Why should the haughty hero boast,
   His vengeful arm, his warlike host!
   While blood defiles his cruel hand,
   And desolation wastes the land.

4. But God beholds and with a frown,
   Casts to the dust his honours down;
   The righteous freed, their hopes recall,
   And hail the proud oppressors fall.

6. We praise the Lord, who heard our cries,
   And sent salvation from the skies;
   The saints, who saw our mournful days,
   Shall join our grateful songs of praise.

Dwight takes that same Biblical Psalm 52 and turns it into words of condemnation for those who speak against Christianity. The subtitle reads "The pride, folly and miserable end, of the Wicked: especially of Infidels." As Dwight's other writings make clear, that term, "Infidels," is not reserved for Muslims (though Dwight refers in stanza three of the next Psalm, 53 Proper Meter, to "Mohammed's empire") or Jews as other writers of the time might have done. "Infidel" could also refer to those in Europe and America who would espouse deism or related systems, the French revolutionists, or even those who simply encouraged a laxity of morals and disestablishment,[12] perhaps even to his former friend, Barlow. He describes the "infidels" thus:

4. Thy law and gospel they despise,
   Vain of their taunts, of madness proud;
   Too rich thy grace to seek, or prize,
   To bow too lofty, even to God.

5. "From ancient days" with scoffs they cry,
   "All things their steadfast course maintain;
   "We see no God in earth, or sky,
   "And find his boasted promise vain."

---

11. Biblical quotations are from the King James Version, which all four authors would have used.

12. See *The Triumph of Infidelity*, especially the last ten pages.

Perhaps the most fascinating part of this Psalm, by one whom the press roundly castigated after the publication of *The Triumph of Infidelity*, is the last two stanzas, where Dwight, as David in the Biblical version, moves into the first person.

11. But in thy courts will I be seen,
     Growing in faith, and hope, and love,
     Like olives' faith, and fresh, and green,
     And ripening for the world above.

12. There will I learn thy glory, Lord,
     And songs for all thy goodness raise;
     There will I wait to hear thy word,
     While listening saints approve the praise.

Obviously, Dwight meant for an entire congregation to sing these words as a statement of faith in orthodoxy over against "infidelity," but they have a particular punch in the first person, a grammatical form Dwight uses sparingly in his transcriptions.

A similar pattern occurs in Barlow's and Dwight's versions of Psalm 59 (missing in Watts). The Biblical Psalm is David's prayer for deliverance from enemies and affirmation of trust in God. Barlow takes the personal prayer and makes it a "Prayer for national deliverance." The content appears to be more physical than spiritual threat.

2. Behold from distant shores,
    And desert wilds they come,
    Combine for blood their barbarous force,
    And through thy cities roam.

3. Beneath the silent shade,
    Their secret plots they lay,
    Our peaceful walls by night invade,
    And waste the fields by day.

Those images could not help but stir memories of both the French and Indian war and the revolutionary war. Again, Dwight turns the Psalm away from the politics of nations and toward the politics of faith. He subtitles the Psalm "Complaints against *Unbelievers*," (italics added).

1. Oh save thy Servants, Lord!
    Fulfill thy gracious word,
    For evil men against us rise;
    Causeless our *souls* they hate;
    Against our lives they wait,
    And aim their malice *at the skies*.

5. They hate thy glory, Lord,
   They mock thy holy word;
   The snares of death their hands employ;
   With flattery, and deceit
   For souls they lie in wait,
   And help the fowler to destroy.

He continues with Psalm 59, second part, titled "Miserable end of the Wicked," which leaves no doubt as to the fate of unbelievers,

4. Just as th'untimely birth
   Returns to moldering earth,
   Or streams in summer pass away,
   So all their dreams of peace,
   And promises of bliss,
   Shall vanish in that dreadful day.

Two other added Psalms reflect political implications. Psalm 79, which in the Bible is a lament of the nation Israel over the conquest of Jerusalem, appears in Barlow as "For the distress of War." Barlow's version is short, simple, and full of moving imagery:

4. Deep from the prison's horrid glooms,
   Oh hear the mournful captives sigh,
   And let thy sovereign power reprieve,
   The trembling souls condemned to die.

Dwight again turns the Psalm to the church, at least partially. His title reads "Complaint of a Nation, or of the Church, Against enemies." The war imagery appears, but so do other allusions:

1. O God attend, while hosts of foes
   Thy heritage invade;
   Thy Salem is become a heap;
   Thy house a ruin made.

3. Behold us, Lord, a remnant sad,
   Of peace and hope forlorn,
   Of every mouth the vile reproach,
   Of every eye the scorn.

7. Help, Lord of hosts, for Jesus' sake,
   The glory of thy name;
   Cleanse us from guilt, our hearts renew,
   And wipe away our shame.

The final added Psalm with political implications is 137, with versions made famous both by Barlow and Dwight. This Psalm had an interesting history in New England; William Billings wrote a paraphrase of the Biblical Psalm during the British occupation of Boston in the American revolution. Using a hermeneutic reminiscent of Watts and his revisers, Billings wrote:

> By the rivers of Watertown we sat down and wept
> When we remember thee, O Boston
>
> . . . .
>
> If I forget thee, O Boston,
> Then let my numbers cease to flow,
> Then be my muse unkind.[13]

Neither Barlow nor Dwight followed Billings' lead, however. Dwight added three settings of the Psalm, including the oldest American hymn still in continuous use, "I Love Thy Kingdom, Lord." Barlow's version stays fairly close to the Biblical Psalm, and he makes his intention clear by subtitling it "The Babylonian Captivity." Dwight's first version also stays close to the Biblical text, but the LM second part he entitles "The Church's Complaint."

> 1. Lord, in these dark and dismal days,
>   We mourn the hidings of thy face;
>   Proud enemies our path surround,
>   To level Zion with the ground.
>
> 2. Her songs, her worship, they deride,
>   And hiss thy word with tongues of pride,
>   And cry, t'insult our humble prayer,
>   "Where is your God, ye Christians, where?"

The original Psalm, and Barlow's paraphrase, speak clearly of political captivity, of a nation being oppressed by another nation. Dwight's version implies that this captivity happens to the church where it is, potentially by the nation inside whose boundaries it exists. In the old tradition of Christian allegorizing of scripture, Dwight has taken the nation Israel and made it not America as happens elsewhere, but the Church within America. The "songs" being derided could refer to the regular practice of some of the presses of printing satires of hymns or Psalms,[14] or, one supposes, it could

13. Cited in Nathaniel Gould, *Church Music in America* (Boston: A. N. Johnson, 1853), 48.

14. For example, in 1798 the *Independent Chronicle* published a poem written at Suffield, Connecticut, which parodied Watts' 148th Psalm and was called "Psalm for a Fast Day"; see Joseph Buckingham, *Specimens of Newspaper Literature*, Vol I (Freeport, NY: Books for Libraries Press, 1971 reprint of 1850 original), 283–4.

refer to Barlow's version of Watts, though Dwight gives no clear indication of that. In any event, the state in this Psalm seems to be put in the role of Babylon to the Church's Israel, a fairly concise statement of Dwight's political and theological position.

Theological Language

Although the alterations due to political language are more obvious and numerous, Barlow and Dwight also revised some language for what might be called theological reasons. These substitutions often deal with a new sensibility about the character of God and of Christ and the use of Biblical language. They also reveal the widening gap between Barlow's emergent deism and Dwight's New Divinity Calvinism.

Thirteen Psalms contain these theological language shifts.[15] Several reflect different emphases in the characterizations of God and Jesus. For example, Barlow, though he shies away from using royal language elsewhere, welcomes it in terms of Jesus. He makes no changes in Watts' usage of this language for Jesus, and in Psalm 2 SM he actually adds it. The Psalm refers to Jesus' actions on behalf of humankind, and Watts' stanza seven begins

> 7. He asks, and God bestows
>   A large inheritance.

Though it does not seem anyone would quibble with such a line, Barlow changes it to read

> 7. Beneath his sovereign sway
>   The Gentile nations bend.

Barlow's understanding of kingship in reference to Christ and God, however, considerably differs from his experience of kingship under Great Britain. Watts paraphrases Psalm 2 LM, stanza nine as

> 9. With humble love address the Son,
>   Lest he grow angry, and ye die:
>   His wrath will burn to worlds unknown,
>   If ye provoke his jealousy.

---

15. Psalms 2 SM, 2 LM, 12 LM, 16 CM 1st, 18 LM 1st, 22 CM 1st, 40 LM, 48 2nd, 53, 58 as 113, 69 LM 2nd, 119 18th, 141 LM (subtitle).

Barlow maintains the first three lines, but softens the picture by closing the stanza with "His love gives life above the sky." He makes a similar, subtle move in Psalm 139 CM first part. The Psalm refers to God, and Watts' stanza four reads

> 4. O! Wondrous knowledge, deep and high!
>   Where can a creature hide?
>   Within thy circling arms I lie,
>   Beset on every side.

Again, Barlow preserves the first three lines, but softens the sense of the fourth by replacing the word "Beset" with "Inclosed." While Watts emphasizes the danger outside, Barlow chooses to emphasize the safety within God's embrace.

The other Christological reference involving Barlow also involves Dwight, and clearly reflects the move in Calvinist theology between Watts' and Dwight's times from a God-centered to a more human-focussed theology. Psalm 69 LM second part begins in Watts

> 1. Twas for thy sake, eternal God
>   Thy Son sustained that heavy load
>   Of base reproach, and sore disgrace,
>   While shame defil'd his sacred face.

Barlow and Dwight both change only the possessive pronoun in line one, Barlow substituting "our" and Dwight "my." In their versions, Christ suffered not for God's sake, but for the salvation of human beings. Dwight moves the Psalm back to the Biblical Psalm's personal mode.

In two other Psalms, Dwight makes changes that neither Mycall nor Barlow make and that refer to God or Christ. One is a minor change; in Psalm 58, "Warning to Magistrates," Dwight changes Watts' second stanza, which reads

> 2. Have ye forgot, or never knew,
>   That God will judge the judges too!

to

> 2. Have ye forgot, or never knew, God is your judge, and he alone?

Considering that Dwight rarely changed Watts without a reason, it seems odd that he did here, unless again he seeks to make a point at once political and theological: God's character is that of judge (which Dwight emphasized more than Watts does) and God *alone* will assess earthly judges who may ignore that fact in their use of power—or who may ignore their lives of faith.

The other unusual change for Dwight involves Christology, again specifically soteriology, and includes the addition of a stanza as well as the change in a stanza. This is the only occasion where the usually conservative Dwight (i.e., conserving what Watts wrote without addition) makes a revision in quite this way. In his version of Psalm 40 LM, Watts tells the story of Christ's sacrifice for our salvation, replacing "bloody" sacrifices. Stanza three reads

> 3. Lo! Thine eternal Son appears!
> To thy desires he bows his ears;
> Assumes a body well prepared
> And well performs a work so hard.

Oddly enough, both Mycall and Barlow paid attention only to the second line. Mycall, in one of the few changes he made that was not clearly grammatical or political, substitutes the word "demands" for "desires" in line two. Barlow chooses instead the word "designs." Dwight changes the whole stanza and then adds a further stanza in the words of Christ:

> 3. In heaven, before his Father's throne
> Complacent, smiles th'eternal Son
> And, pleased, presents with boundless grace
> Himself, a ransom for our race.
>
> 4. "Mine ear is open'd to thy voice,
> My heart delighted with thy choice;
> Pleas'd, I assume a fleshy form,
> Akin to man, that dying worm."

Why make a change that seems to alter so little in Watts' intent? Dwight's version makes Christ's salvific work even more prominent than Watts' (overtly using the theological atonement concept of "ransom") as he and Barlow did in Psalm 69 (above). The image of the "dying worm," which startles and seems out of place coming from the lips of Jesus in this Psalm, sounds like a throw-back to the strong Calvinism of Dwight's grandfather, or to a Biblical image. Dwight was fond of the return to Biblical imagery, and this may have contributed to the change. On the other hand, Berk spoke of Dwight "humanizing" orthodox Calvinism.[16] Could Dwight here

---

16. Stephen Berk, *Calvinism versus Democracy: Timothy Dwight and the Origins of American Evangelical Orthodoxy* (Hamden, Connecticut: Archon Books, 1974), 80.

be emphasizing Jesus' humanity ("fleshy form," kinship with humanity) as a hopeful word to those who would sing this Psalm?

Whether or not that was the case, Dwight elsewhere made the move toward restoring Biblical language to Watts but more especially to Barlow, and some of the changes—and changes back from Barlow to Watts' original version—in Dwight reflect this concern. In Psalm 22 CM, first part, for example, Watts uses the Biblical image from the prophets "As Bulls of Bashan fierce and strong" in stanza seven, line three. Barlow seeks to bring that image into a more understandable word for people of his time. He writes the line "By foes encompass'd fierce and strong." In his version, Dwight reclaims Watts' original Biblical image. The same thing occurs in Psalm 48 SM, second part, where Watts begins stanza two with the line "With joy let Judah stand," and Barlow writes "With joy thy people stand." Dwight uses Watts' form. This example also shows Barlow's occasional tendency move from specific to a more universal reference. He makes a similar alteration in Psalm 53, stanza four, lines three and four, which read in Watts:

> 4. Jacob with all his tribes shall sing,
>   And Judah weep no more.

Barlow's version reads:

> 4. Thy joyful saints thy praise shall sing,
>   And Israel weep no more.

He retains the Biblical language of "Israel," but that term, as in "the new Israel," occurred in millennial speech in reference to America, so it would not be as specific as "Judah."

Perhaps the oddest division of opinion among Barlow, Dwight, and Watts on Biblical language comes in the case of Psalms 35 and 41. In these Psalms Watts uses the word "bowels" to refer to compassion, mercy or tenderness, as is done in the Old Testament.[17] Barlow's sense of the changes in language moved him to change both references as follows:

> Psalm 35 CM, second stanza, line three
> Watts: Hark how his sounding bowels move,

---

17. See, for example, Jeremiah 31:20, Psalm 22:14, Psalm 109:18, or Lamentations 1:20 or 2:11 among others in the King James Version. For more on the Hebrew understanding of which emotions resided in which parts of the body, see Hans Walter Wolff, *The Anthropology of the Old Testament* (Philadelphia: Fortress, 1974), especially 63–64.

Barlow: Behold his kind compassion move.
Psalm 41, stanza one, line one
  Watts: Blest is the man whose bowels move
      And melt with pity to the poor.
  Barlow: Blest is the man, whose breast can move
      And melt with pity to the poor.
Psalm 41, stanza two, lines three and four
  Watts: He, in the time of general grief
      Shall find the Lord has bowels, too.
  Barlow: He in the time of general grief
      Shall find the Lord hath mercy, too.

In every case, Dwight erased the Barlow changes and went back to the Watts/Biblical (specifically King James) language. In this case, that move seems a strange one, given the fact that this Psalter was meant for congregational singing and not study. This strange non-change by Dwight reveals the deep streak in his political, theological, and social sensibilities of conserving the imagery, if not all the substance, of the past. His pastoral poetry paints a picture of the ideal, safe, traditional community of Greenfield Hill where, at the same time, he operated a co-educational academy against all tradition. This facet of Dwight appears more than once in his version of Watts.

Finally, the revisions that reflect theological matters reveal, as noted above, Barlow's move away from the orthodox Calvinism of his youth toward the deism, or at least humanistic Calvinism, of his later life. The universalizing tendency already noted may be a piece of this turn of his thought. This may best be shown in the change of the subtitle to Psalm 141 LM from Watts' "Watchfulness and Brotherly Reproof" to Barlow's "Watchfulness and Brotherly Love." The change may seem insignificant—not even in words that are sung—but the theological stress on love rather than reproof illustrates a considerable shift on Barlow's part. The same tendency is revealed more subtly in Psalm 16 CM, first part. Watts writes in stanza two:

> 2. Yet if my God prolong my breath,
>   The saints may profit by it;
>   The saints, the glory of the earth
>   The men of my delight.

Barlow is less concerned with the saints profiting by his prolonged life.

> 2. Yet if my God prolong my breath,
>   The saints may still rejoice;

The saints, the glory of the earth
The people of my choice.

Dwight also makes a change in this stanza, but instead of the people of his choice rejoicing, he explicitly turns the words into those of a faithful pastor, as in "Greenfield Hill":

2. Yet here thy children to sustain
   Shall be my lov'd employ,
   Thy children, first and best of men
   My friends, my highest joy.

The added Psalms reveal few dramatic theological differences between Barlow and Dwight. For the most part, they reflect the difference between the two men's theological vehemence. Barlow's added Psalms stay fairly close to the Biblical themes and are usually considerably shorter than Dwight's. Barlow also tends toward the general while Dwight goes for the specific.

Psalms 28 LM and 43 illustrate these directions. The Biblical Psalm 28 is a cry to God for help against evil influences, both on an individual and "thy people" (KJV). Barlow preserves that form in a five-stanza, straightforward piece that asks for help both for an individual and, in the last line, for "thy church." Dwight, on the other hand, produces an eleven-stanza piece that goes into some detail about those who threaten the godly and God's ultimate treatment of both evil and good.

4. While peace their flattering lips proclaim,
   And love profess, and hope impart,
   They blast their neighbour's first part fame,
   And wing their arrows to his heart.[18]

5. But, while they plant the secret snare,
   Thy searching eyes their path regard,
   Thy hands their dreadful doom prepare,
   And mete their guilt its just reward.

The rest of the Psalm is a trope on these two stanzas.

Psalm 43 displays the same principle on a slightly different theme. The Biblical Psalm again is a personal plea to God for deliverance and profession of faith, and is quite short. Barlow even quotes the first line of the Psalm in the King James Version to begin his Psalm. The rest is an extremely close, brief (five stanzas, matching the Biblical five verses) paraphrase of the King James translation.

---

18. Could this be a comment on his literary and theological critics?

Dwight, however, whose original charge urged him to pare down Barlow's excessive changes, departs considerably both from Barlow and the Bible in a seven-stanza song in Proper Meter (i.e., 6666 4444). He subtitles the Psalm "A complaint, mingled with hope, under great trials, particularly, long detention from public worship," thus making the subject much more specific than the Biblical writer. Because the importance of public worship (and government support thereof) stood paramount in his battle against "infidelity," amorality, and a host of other problems besetting the early republic, the specific message of this Psalm makes sense. One wonders if he had his parish in Greenfield Hill in mind when writing stanza six:

6. Then in thy holy hill
   Before thine altar, Lord,
   My harp and song shall sound
   The glories of thy word.
       Henceforth to thee,
       O God of grace,
       A hymn of praise
       My life shall be.

On two occasions, the subject each writer chooses for the Psalm's point of view reflects the theological differences between Dwight and Barlow. If the Biblical Psalm is a personal subject, Barlow usually retains that point of view. Psalms 88 and 108 illustrate this point. Dwight, however, moves the subject in 88, which he splits into four extremely long parts, from Jesus in part one, to humankind as a whole in parts two and three, and finally to the personal in part four. The Biblical Psalm's point of view is that of an individual, as Barlow retains it, and expresses the fears of one who is dying and feeling abandoned by God. Dwight again makes the classic hermeneutical move of placing those words in the mouth of Christ:

8. Though friend and lover, near and dear,
   In dark recesses hide;
   Though here I meet the darts of hate,
   And bear the scoffs of pride;

9. I'll lift my hands, I'll raise my eyes,
   For thy salvation, Lord:
   Thy hand shall save me from my foes,
   And well fulfill thy word.

Dwight then adds a footnote referring to Vitringa and Bishop Horne, who used this same interpretation of the Psalm. One

assumes Dwight wanted to show historical precedent for his paraphrase.

Parts two and three present a classic formulation of Calvinist salvation theology with a decidedly revivalistic call to "get right with
God." Part three, stanza two, reads:

> 2. While God invites, how blessed the day!
>   How sweet the gospel's charming sound!
>   "Come sinners, haste, oh haste away,
>   While yet a pardoning God he's found."

The emotional tone of this text is somewhat surprising for the man
who later condemned the overly emotional versions of the Great
Awakening revivals, but seems consistent with his vehemence concerning the need for a revival at Yale. That emotional tone becomes
accentuated to an even greater degree in the fourth part, "Solemn
thoughts, after dangerous sickness." This song carries the familiar
themes of the death bed and re-evaluation of one's life, reminiscent
of John Donne's "Holy Sonnet one" of 1633, or "Hymn to God
My God in My Sickness" of 1635 (though not of the same literary
quality). In keeping with the revivalistic tone of the piece, he adds
these last two stanzas:

> 12. Ye sinners, fear the Lord,
>   While yet tis called to day;
>   Soon will the awful voice of death
>   Command your souls away.

> 13. Soon will the harvest close;
>   The summer soon be o'er;
>   And soon your injured angry God
>   Will hear your prayers no more.

Dwight's Edwardsian ancestry meets the Second Great Awakening
in these lines.

Psalm 108 in the Bible expresses both a personal and national call
for deliverance and song of praise to God. Barlow, in a short four
stanzas, chooses to stress the praise and the individual singer's point
of view, "Awake, my soul, to sound his praise,/Awake my harp to
sing . . .," while Dwight moves quickly from the individual point of
view to that of the church and its call to God to defend it against all
foes. This theme by now is familiar to Dwight's readers. It becomes
a clarion call for the church to stand against those who contend
with it.

9. Save us from sin, and fear, and woe,
   From every snare and every foe,
   And help us boldly to contend,
   Falsehood resist, and truth defend.

One last theological theme relevant to Dwight's time appears in these added Psalms. As was noted above, Dwight used some of the profits of his volume to benefit the nascent missionary movement in the United States. His version of Psalm 53 in Proper Meter, which he adds to Watts' existing versions, is clearly a call to mission. The last two lines of stanza one read:

1. Oh let thy Spirit like soft dews descend;
   Thy Gospel run to earth's remotest end.

Stanza four gives the theme a distinctly American slant:

4. In barren wilds shall living waters spring;
   Fair temples rise, and songs of transport ring;
   The savage mind with sweet affections warm,
   And light and love, the yielding bosom charm;
   From sin's oblivious sleep the soul arise,
   And grace, and goodness, shower from balmy skies.

The Psalm ends on a note reminiscent of Watts' version of Psalm 72 (which Dwight retains unaltered), "Jesus shall reign where'er the sun . . ." Dwight's last line reads "And Jesus spread his reign from sea to sea," again a specific allusion to the American missionary situation. The closest Barlow comes to any clear missionary theme (writing fifteen years before Dwight) comes in Psalm 54 CM, stanza four, line three, "Extend thy truth through every land," a somewhat less forceful piece than the Dwight.

Miscellany

A staggering one hundred and fifty-six of Watts' "imitations" were changed for a variety of largely aesthetic reasons by Mycall, Barlow, or Dwight individually or, in some rare cases, by two or all three. Without doubt, as Ezra Stiles observed, Barlow made the great majority of the changes. In addition to those Psalms revised for political and theological reasons mentioned above, Barlow made other changes to one hundred and thirty-five of Watts' texts. By contrast,

Mycall amended twenty-five Watts Psalms[19] and Dwight made thirty-three changes that had no political or theological rationale.

The reasoning behind Mycall's choices proves hard to discern because so little is known about his motives for producing the Psalter, other than Stiles' comments on the need to change the political language. One might assume that because Mycall was a businessman the market determined to some extent what he re-wrote. Most of his emendations made the Psalms flow more smoothly and therefore easier to sing to some of the new tunes being produced. For example, in Psalm 95 LM, stanza four, line two, Mycall changes Watts' "Tempted their maker to his face," to "Yet tempt their maker to his face." The change in which syllable gets stressed makes a difference in how easily it fits to any given tune. Barlow retains Mycall's change while Dwight prefers the Watts version. Mycall makes a similar change for ease of line flow in Psalm 115. Watts writes in stanza one, line three, "Eternal God, thou'rt only just." Clearly that odd contraction could be difficult to get out of a singer's mouth. Mycall makes it "Eternal God! Thou only just." Barlow agrees with Mycall; Dwight sees the problem but corrects it differently: " 'Tis thine, great God, the only just." Of course Watts' original intent in producing his *Imitation* was to make the Psalms more singable, so his American revisers merely continued toward that goal.

The vast majority of these miscellaneous revisions by all three authors seem to reflect a desire for a smoother, more easily sung text. A few, however, are more interesting for a variety of reasons. Barlow, in keeping perhaps with his developing humanism or simply his sense of what is appropriate poetically for worship, softens Watts' occasionally harsh imagery.[20] In Psalm 6 CM, stanza five, Watts writes about God listening to prayer, "He hears when dust and ashes speak." Barlow mutes that coarse view of humankind to "He hears his mourning children speak." In Psalm 39 CM, third part, Barlow omits Watts' entire fifth stanza:

> 5. This mortal life decays apace,
>   How soon the bubble's broke!
>   Adam, and all his numerous race
>   Are vanity and smoke.

---

19. The number refers to significant changes. Mycall had habit of making myriad grammatical changes in tense, etc., which had little impact on the meaning of the text and, for the most part, disappeared in subsequent editions.

20. Undoubtedly those who have studied Barlow's poetry at some length could provide commentary on similarities in style between his Psalms and his other poems, but this lies beyond the scope of this study.

In 49 LM, stanza four, line two, Barlow changes Watts' "Laid in the grave for worms to eat" to "And leave his glories in the tomb." Finally, in Psalm 129 CM, Watts writes:

3. Their cruel plough had torn my flesh
   With furrows long and deep,
   Hourly they vexed my wounds afresh,
   Nor let my sorrows sleep.

Barlow amends that sharp, physical imagery to read:

3. O'er all my frame their cruel dart
   Its painful wounds impressed
   Hourly they vexed my fainting heart,
   Nor let my sorrows rest.

Barlow still gets the point across but mutes the graphic imagery of Watts. Without exception, Dwight restores Watts' original language in these Psalms. The grandson of Edwards and one of the catalysts behind the second Great Awakening had no problem with graphic imagery in worship.

A second interesting pattern in Barlow appears in the subtitles of the individual Psalms, particularly in what Barlow leaves out. Psalm 107, last part, in Watts carried the subtitle "A Psalm for New England." Watts' Psalm concerns the faithful going to a barren place "Where nothing dwelt but beasts of prey,/Or men as fierce and wild as they," and how God prospers these new cities and settlements. It may be that Watts included this to help gain a market in pre-revolutionary New England. Mycall keeps Psalm and subtitle unaltered, as does Dwight. Barlow, though, perhaps not wanting to celebrate the colonizer so soon after the colonies gained their freedom, keeps the text of the Psalm as Watts, but drops the subtitle. A later version of Barlow in 1814 adds a subtitle "Colonies planted or Nations blessed or punished." A similar occurrence is found in Psalm 119, the eighth, ninth, and seventeenth parts, where Barlow leaves out all or part of Watts' subtitle while later editors add their own.

One last Barlow emendation that merits comment happens in Psalm 8 paraphrased. In stanza two, Watts writes

2. To thee the voices of the young
   A monument of honor raise.

Mycall and Dwight see no problem with this, but Barlow changes that second line to "Their sounding notes of honour raise." Can it be significant that Barlow preferred the overt musical imagery of "notes" to the more permanent, stony image of "monument"? In the New England of his time, were there many "monuments" in place?

Dwight's miscellaneous changes, while more numerous than his Preface might lead one to believe, seem to be simple poetic disagreements with Watts. It may be significant that, despite the public outrage of the Connecticut divines against Barlow, Dwight more than once (in seventeen texts) agrees with Barlow on the need to change a line of poetry, though they usually approach the revisions differently. One exception to that seems to be Psalm 71 CM, second part, stanza six, line four, where both Dwight and Barlow change Watts' line "And drown'd them in his blood" to "And saved me by his blood." It appears the two men could agree on an atonement theology if nothing else.

Except in the occasional anthology, both Dwight's and Barlow's poetry exerted little lasting influence on American literature. Did these Psalters meet the same fate? The next chapter explores the lasting influence of all three revisers' Psalm texts in the life of the American churches.

Chapter Six

Who Used What When: The Choreography of Worship

Lawrence Hoffman, in his method of studying liturgical change, suggests looking at text and context, and also at what he calls "choreography."[1] Hoffman means by this, "the way services are conducted." Hoffman had the advantage of both written descriptions and human memory for his study. For New England Congregational churches in the first half of the nineteenth century, neither human memory nor written descriptions prove particularly helpful. As Dwight had written in *Greenfield Hill*, worship had become "habit" for New Englanders,[2] and they did not write at length about its details.

The search to determine the usage of the revised and new texts of Mycall, Barlow, and Dwight, then, must rely on a variety of sources and imaginative reconstruction. The story is told primarily through three media: local church and town histories, tunebooks, and subsequent Psalters. These illustrate to some extent which of the revisions and new texts were retained well into the new century and how they were used in public worship. From these sources one can begin to discern the ultimate impact of this liturgical change at the close of the eighteenth century on subsequent New England worshipers.

Local Church and Town Histories

The vast bulk of the material from published local church and town histories concerns clergy biography and recitations of conflict or

---

1. Lawrence Hoffman, *Beyond the Text* (Bloomington: Indiana University Press, 1987), 71.

2. Timothy Dwight, *Greenfield Hill*, in William McTaggart and William Bottorff, eds, *The Major Poems of Timothy Dwight* (Gainesville, Florida: Scholars' Facsimiles and Reprints, 1969), 494.

political matters within congregations, as well as records of building
issues. When the writers turn to worship, most often they write
about sermons, as befits the fact that the sermon stood at the liturgical and emotional center of New England Congregational worship
throughout the eighteenth and nineteenth centuries.

O. E. Daggett, writing in 1846, noted that "many of the Congregational and Presbyterian churches in this country still sing no
Psalms but his [Watts'] allowing no changes in these . . . (excepting
national allusions,) . . . ."[3] The church histories confirm this dedication to Watts. South Church in Andover, Massachusetts, presents a
good example of this. In 1772, the congregation voted

> to sing Dr. Watts's Psalms and Hymns, three months. For eighty-
> seven years, then, the people have sung, for the most part, these songs
> of Zion, the only changes since being the gradual introduction, in ad-
> dition, of the Select Hymns of Dr. Worcester.[4]

Similar stories come from First Church in Newton, Massachusetts,
which used Watts until 1871, and First Church in Cambridge, Massachusetts, which in 1817 went from Tate and Brady to Watts'
Psalms and Hymns.[5]

Perhaps the most interesting testimonial to the power of Watts
comes in a work of fiction based on fact. Samuel Gilman, born in
1791, wrote what he called a fictitious memoir of life in a New England church choir at the turn of the nineteenth century in New
Hampshire. Gilman's book provides an interesting window on
music in New England churches. He tells the story of a minister
starting the congregation on a hymn from the "second book" of
Dr. Watts' (presumably *Psalms and Hymns*) that the bulk of the
communing members did not like. The church voted in a require-
ment that the minister begin at the beginning of Watts' Psalter the
next Sunday and sing every verse of the Psalms in order throughout
the year. Gilman comments that "Watts, like the Common Prayer
Book in the Church of England, receiv[ed] in many parts of this
region an equal reverence with the Bible."[6]

---

3. O. E. Daggett, "The Psalms in Worship," *The New Englander*, July
1846: 326.

4. *Historical Manual of the South Church in Andover, Massachusetts*
(Andover: Warren Draper, 1859), 56.

5. *The Commemorative Services of the First Church in Newton, Massachusetts on the Occasion of the Two Hundred and Twenty-Fifth Anniversary
of its Foundation* (Boston: Rockwell and Churchill, 1890), 170; Alexander
McKenzie, *Lectures on the History of the First Church in Cambridge* (Boston: Congregational Publishing Society, 1873), 186.

6. Samuel Gilman, *Memoirs of a New England Village Choir with Occasional Reflections* (Boston: S. G. Goodrich 1829), 145.

Knowing that at least three revisions of Watts circulated in New England, the question arises as to which Watts these churches used. Rarely do histories note the use of a specific revision, although publishing records certainly indicate they were used. It was not the established practice of the time, either in hymn books or tunebooks, to indicate the author of any particular hymn, let alone the reviser. The reader would assume that a piece was unadulterated Watts, which lent a hymn or Psalm greater respectability than to have Mycall's, Barlow's, or even Dwight's name associated with it. Without knowing the publisher and date of any congregation's Watts, it remains impossible to know which Watts they used.

Occasionally, however, a specific reference is made. *The History of New London Connecticut* contains a brief note that in 1806 Abel McEwen was called as Pastor to the Congregational church there. His ordination sermon was preached by Timothy Dwight, and, "with Mr. McEwen's ministry, Dwight's Psalms and Hymns were introduced."[7] A similar reference occurs in the history of the First Church in Hartford, Connecticut.

> In 1799, moved by the impulse of desire for a class of hymns better adapted to the happy "revival of religion" which characterized the period, Dr. Strong published a hymnbook known as *The Hartford Selection of Hymns* .... Presumably it must have been used in Dr. Strong's own congregation, but it is in evidence that as early as 1812 the compilation made at the request of the General Association of Connecticut by President Dwight, in 1800, was employed in this Society.[8]

First Church in Hartford continued to use Dwight's Watts until 1845, though a vote was taken in 1836 to substitute *The Christian Psalmist*.[9] The pattern in Connecticut of moving from one official Psalter to the next appears in the records of the Church of Christ (Congregational) of Norfolk, Connecticut. In describing worship in the late eighteenth century, the historian notes "The minister announced the psalm and read it; probably from Barlow's *Psalm Book*

---

7. Frances Manwaring Caulkins, *History of New London, Connecticut* (New London: Published by the author, 1852), 590.

8. George Leon Walker, *History of the First Church in Hartford 1633–1883* (Hartford: Brown and Gross, 1884), 348–49.

9. Ibid., 394. Benson notes that there is no evidence that *The Hartford Selection*, a more revivalist hymnbook, was ever actually used in public worship in the churches of Hartford, as opposed to revival meetings. Louis F. Benson, *The English Hymn* (Richmond: John Knox, 1915), 373.

[sic], the earliest of which there is mention."[10] In 1804 the church replaced Barlow with Dwight, and in 1845 Dwight's Watts "was succeeded by *Psalms and Hymns of the General Association*," the follow-up to Dwight in Connecticut (see below).[11] In the history of the Second Church in Hartford, notice is taken of the publication of Barlow's Psalter, but the author does not indicate if the church made use of it.[12]

Finally, a cryptic, intriguing note appears in the Diary of William Bentley, a pastor of East Church in Salem, Massachusetts. He records that on Independence Day in 1806, the town celebrated "with Old Hundred in an accommodated Psalm from Dr. Watts."[13] The question of whose "accommodation" of Watts remains unanswered.

Despite a scarcity of specific reference to any of the revisions by name, the church histories, the 1846 article by Daggett, and Benson's works tell of the churches' use of subsequent collections that contained many of the revised versions of Watts, especially by Barlow and Dwight. Worcester's various collections, Lowell Mason's 1831 *Church Psalmody*, and the General Association of Connecticut's 1845 *Psalms and Hymns for Christian use and worship*, all featured, as noted below, significant pieces of Barlow and Dwight. Churches in Ridgefield, Connecticut, Bennington, Vermont, and Fall River, Massachusetts, among others, all record the use of Mason's *Church Psalmody*.[14] Worcester's "Watts and Select" found extensive use, especially in Massachusetts (Salem and Braintree, for example),[15] and, in addition to the notation from Norfolk above, the General Association's Psalter was used in places such as the Second Church in Hartford.[16]

---

10. James H. Potter, *Church of Christ (Congregational) Norfolk, Connecticut Two Hundred Years* (Norfolk: [n.p.], 1960), 31.

11. Ibid., 54 and 67.

12. Edwin Pond Parker, *History of the Second Church of Christ in Hartford* (Hartford: Belknap and Warfield, 1892), 150.

13. William Bentley, *The Diary of William Bentley D.D.* (Gloucester, Massachusetts: Peter Smith, 1962), Vol. III, 238.

14. Muriel R. Hanson, *A History of the First Congregational Church of Ridgefield 1712-1962* (Ridgefield: The Church, 1962), 34; Isaac Jennings, *The One Hundred Year Old Meetinghouse of the Church of Christ in Bennington, Vermont* (Cambridge, Mass: Riverside Press, 1907), 54; Mrs. William Carr et al., *History, Annals and Sketches of the Central Church of Fall River, Massachusetts* (Boston: Fort Hill Press, 1905), 8. Mrs. Carr notes that Mason's book was "the most approved collection of psalmody in all our churches. . . ."

15. Bentley, *Diary*, Vol. III, 61; Ruth W. Shuster, *Gathered in 1707* (Braintree, Mass: First Congregational Church, 1957), 99.

16. Edwin Pond Parker, *History of the Second Church of Christ in Hartford*, 235.

Tunebooks

Before exploring the later Psalm collections, we can examine the choreography of the liturgical change brought about by Watts' revisers by looking at tunebooks of the period. The tunebooks are one piece of a larger change in the general choreography of worship. They arose from the introduction of choirs into public worship and the transformation in the manner of singing that had occurred earlier in the eighteenth century.

As noted in chapter three, the middle of the eighteenth century in New England brought a great controversy concerning the method of singing in public worship. The earliest New England settlers sang the "usual" way; a precentor lined out the Psalms, which the congregation repeated line by line. As time passed and memories of tunes became even more limited, as congregations spread and trained musicians were fewer and farther between, this singing degenerated, at least in the opinion of many clergymen. It was time for a change.

In 1721, two New England musicians led the charge for what came to be called "regular" singing: not line by line but the whole congregation singing together through a Psalm, in parts when possible. John Tuft's *Introduction to the Singing of Psalm Tunes* and Thomas Walter's *The Grounds and Rules of Musick* called for a revival of congregational singing, for the introduction of part singing, and for the establishment of "singing schools" to train church members how to sing.[17] Prominent divines such as Cotton Mather supported this effort, and despite objection from more conservative churches, the "regular" way of singing gained in popularity. The first Great Awakening hastened this process, as church members felt a call to sing and the hymnody of Isaac Watts began to appear in America. This brought numerous changes to music in public worship; indeed Marini claims "regular singing clearly democratized Congregationalist Psalmody and brought women their first significant liturgical role . . . ."[18]

This new excitement about congregational singing also produced a need for new music suited to new hymns and to a new fervor among singers. In 1770, William Billings published *The New-England Psalm-Singer: or, the American Chorister*,[19] which was the first of many tunebooks to come from American publishers after

---

17. Stephen Marini, "Rehearsal for Revival: Sacred Singing and the Great Awakening," in *Sacred Sound: Music in Religious Thought and Practice*, Joyce Irwin, ed. (Chico, California: Scholar's Press, 1983), 73.

18. Ibid., 76.

19. Boston: Edes and Gill, 1770.

the revolution. The tunebooks met the needs of the singing schools, which were providing churches with small groups of highly trained singers clamoring for seats set aside in church to lead the music of worship. This era saw the birth of the American volunteer church choir that would, before long, come to dominate singing in many churches as had the precentors a generation before.

In 1779, South Church in Andover voted to add seats in the sanctuary for the choir.[20] Choirs likewise came to Hampstead, New Hampshire, in 1767, to Shirley, Massachusetts, in 1786, to Wellesley in 1798, to East Haven, Connecticut, in 1799, and to First Church, Cambridge, in 1817 (the same year the church went from Tate and Brady to Watts).[21]

Gilman's *Memoirs* record that at one time the choir in his pseudo-fictional New Hampshire church numbered fifty members, that they sang five times a Sunday, and implies that they sang in place of the congregation.[22] He also mentions one tunebook used by the choir by name: *The Village Harmony*.[23]

The Village Harmony is one of the tunebooks Richard Crawford lifts up in his study of the core repertory of American Psalm tunes.[24] Crawford identified the one hundred and one tunes that appear most often in American tunebooks and the texts most frequently

---

20. *Historical Manual*, 56.

21. Harriette Eliza Noyes, *A Memorial History of Hampstead New Hampshire Congregational Church, 1752–1902* , Vol. II (Boston: George Reed, 1903), 167; Seth Chandler, *History of the Town of Shirley Massachusetts* (Shirley: Published by the Author, 1883), 227; Edward Herrick Chandler, *The History of the Wellesley Congregational Church* (Boston: Benjamin H. Sanborn, 1898), 40; Henry Kelso Eversull, *The Evolution of an Old New England Church* (East Haven: Tuttle, Morehouse and Taylor, 1924), 76; McKenzie, *First Church in Cambridge*, 187. The East Haven history notes the choir was all male.

22. Gilman, *Memoirs*, 26, 95, 40.

23. Ibid., 13. The tunebooks would have been only in the hands of the choirs, not the congregation as a whole. It is possible, however, that members of the congregation, as well as the choir, held the Psalters in hand. Early in the nineteenth century, a pastor in Cambridge, Massachusetts, preached a sermon in which he exhorted the congregation, if they had no gift for singing, to listen to others and "keep their eyes fixed on the psalm or hymn that is sung, and join with the understanding and affections in the sublime employment, and thus make melody, at least in their hearts, to the Lord." McKenzie, *First Church in Cambridge*, 187.

24. Richard Crawford, *The Core Repertory of Early American Psalmody* (Madison: A-R Editions, 1984). Crawford confines the core repertory to the years 1761–1810. Inclusion in the core repertory is based solely on the frequency of the printings of a tune.

associated with those tunes. He also identifies which tunebooks carried the most of these core tunes. With the rise of the choir and the composition of so much new American music sung in churches, these tunebooks become important sources for discerning which texts of Watts and the revisions the churches regularly sang before and after the turn of the century.

The challenge of these sources is that in most tunebooks only the first line or stanza of a text is reproduced. The great bulk of the revisions of Watts come in subsequent stanzas. Therefore one cannot readily tell exactly which version of Watts the choir and congregation held in hand.

These tunebooks do contain tantalizing hints of at least a few of the revisions that made an impact on choirs and congregations. *The Village Harmony*, for example, which contains 62 (1803 edition) or 63 (1807 edition) core repertory tunes, includes the tune OCEAN, as do many tunebooks of the period.[25] The text most often associated with this tune, according to Crawford, is Watts' Psalm 107, fourth part.[26] In this tunebook, as in others (including *Federal Harmony* of 1792 and *United States Sacred Harmony* of 1799,[27]), the version printed is not pure Watts, but Barlow's revision of stanza one, lines two and four. Significantly, this Psalm is not one of those with British references, but simply one of Barlow's aesthetic changes which seem to have stuck.

An earlier tunebook, *The Chorister's Companion* in its 1788 second edition,[28] does take note of one of those changes in political language. Its version of Psalm 100, to the tune GRATITUDE, uses John Mycall's revision of stanza one, line three, from Watts' "The British Isles shall send the noise," to Mycall's "America shall send the noise." Later tunebooks and Psalters most often use Barlow's re-writing of this entire stanza (see further below).

The information most often gleaned from these tunebooks concerns which of the new texts (i.e., the twelve Psalms omitted by Watts but included by Barlow and Dwight) became popular enough to be associated with an oft-sung tune and printed in a tunebook.

---

25. *The Village Harmony or Youth's Assistant to Sacred Music*, 6th and 8th editions (Exeter, New Hampshire: Norris and Sawyer, 1803 and 1807), 72.

26. Crawford, *Core Repertory*, 105.

27. *The Federal Harmony* (Boston: John Norman, 1792), 34; Amos Pilsbury, *The United States Sacred Harmony* (Boston: Isaiah Thomas and Ebenezer Andrews, 1799), 22.

28. *The Chorister's Companion* (New Haven: Simeon Jocelin, 1788), 61. This book contains 37 core repertory tunes.

Individual instances of two or three occur, including Dwight's rendition of Psalm 54 and Barlow's of Psalm 88.[29] The most common appearances of the added Psalms, however, are of both Dwight's and Barlow's versions of Psalm 137. Barlow's paraphrase, "Along the banks where Babel's current flows," continued to be praised for its literary merit long after his death. A writer as late as 1873 lauded it as remaining "to this day without a rival."[30] Several tunebooks carried Barlow's paraphrase of 137 to a variety of tunes including BABYLON, PERGAMUS, and DESPONDENCE.[31] Dwight's third version of the Psalm, "I love thy kingdom, Lord," the one that remains in hymnals today, appeared less often in early tunebooks. It did appear in the 1840 *Massachusetts Collection* to the tune WESTWOOD.[32] It is important to remember, however, that each tune in any tunebook had numerous texts which might be sung to them, at the discretion of clergy, choir leaders, and choir members. Without more detailed records, it remains impossible to tell solely from tunebooks which of the revised texts continued in use into the nineteenth century.

Subsequent Psalters

Perhaps a better clue than the tunebooks offer comes to modern researchers from the New England Psalters that appeared after 1801. An exploration of the texts appearing in the most popular Psalters of the first half of the nineteenth century yields some surprising results, especially in regard to the staying power of Barlow's supposedly "tainted" texts.

Examining local church histories and relying on the research of

29. The Barlow appears in Samuel Holyoke, *The Christian Harmonist* (Salem, Massachusetts: Joshua Cushing, 1804), 140. ENFIELD is one of the core repertory tunes, but Crawford notes that except in this and one other book, the tune is usually associated with another text; Crawford, *Core Repertory*, xxxv. The Dwight appears in F.D. Allen, *The New York Selection of Sacred Music* (New York: Bartlett and Raynor, 1833), 106. This also is a core repertory tune that seems to have been associated with several texts.

30. Anonymous, "Joel Barlow," *The New Englander*, July 1873: 417. A similar sentiment is found in Rufus Griswold, *The Poets and Poetry of America* (Philadelphia: Carey and Hart, 1843), 24, where Griswold describes this Psalm paraphrase as "the finest translation of the words of David that has been written."

31. See Pilsbury, *United States*, 1799, 129; Holyoke, *Christian Harmonist*, 1804, 156 and George James Webb, *The Massachusetts Collection of Psalmody* (Boston: Crocker and Brewster, 1840), 149.

32. Webb, *Massachusetts Collection*, 129.

Louis Benson, four Psalters appear to have been used most often in New England churches through the first half of the century: Samuel Worcester's 1819 *Psalms, Hymns and Spiritual Songs of the Rev. Isaac Watts,* which became more popularly known as "Watts and Select," Lowell Mason's 1831 *Church Psalmody,* Hastings and Patton's 1836 *The Christian Psalmist,* and the official sequel to Dwight's work for the General Association of Connecticut which was published in 1845 as *Psalms and Hymns for Christian Use and Worship.* A comparison of each of those Psalters in turn with the revised Watts of the previous century sheds light on what congregations continued to value for their church music.

Without question, the Second Great Awakening that followed the growing popularity in the United States of Watts' and Wesley's hymns, among others, lifted the art of English hymnody into prominence, threatening the hegemony of Psalms in public worship. Nevertheless many congregations, especially in rural New England, continued to place Psalms as the most important pieces to be sung in worship. South Church in Andover, Massachusetts, illustrates this. The church historian writes that, after a 1772 vote to sing Watts' *Psalms and Hymns,* "for eighty-seven years the people have sung, for the most part, these songs of Zion, the only changes since being the gradual introduction, in addition, of the Select Hymns of Dr. Worcester."[33]

This continuing desire on the part of clergy and lay people to sing Psalms resulted in a market for new versions of the Psalter, or at least of Watts. Samuel Worcester of Salem, Massachusetts, first decided to enter this market with an 1815 Watts revision that met with great criticism and little commercial success.[34] At the urging of his publisher, Worcester dropped that volume and "enlarged the selection of hymns it contained, and . . . appended them to the complete *Psalms and Hymns* of Watts."[35] Benson's implication here is that Worcester did away with all his unpopular revisions and gave the public Watts pristine. That, however, is not the case.

The volume that came popularly to be known as "Watts and Select"[36] contained many fewer changes than either Worcester's

---

33. *Historical Manual,* 56.

34. *Christian Psalmody in four parts; comprising Dr. Watts's Psalms abridged; Dr. Watts's Hymns abridged; select hymns from other authors; and select Harmony* (Boston: 1815).

35. Benson, *English Hymn,* 168.

36. The complete title was *The Psalms, Hymns and Spiritual Songs of the Rev. Isaac Watts, D.D. to which are added Select Hymns from other authors* (Boston: Samuel Armstrong). The original edition came out in 1819, with revisions in 1823 and 1834. The text used for comparison in this study is the 1823 revision.

previous effort or Barlow's or Dwight's editions. In a few of the
Psalms, Worcester made his own changes. For example, Psalm 97
CM, first stanza, first line, reads in Watts, "Ye Islands of the Northern sea." Both Barlow and Dwight change the line, which is a clear
reference to Great Britain. Worcester adopts neither the Barlow nor
the Dwight version, but uses instead "Ye shores and isles of ev'ry
sea." He makes his own changes also in Psalms 100 LM, second
part, Psalm 60 CM, Psalm 96 PM, and Psalm 136 CM. In several
places where either Barlow or Dwight made changes, Worcester retains the original Watts, as in Psalm 91 LM, first part, stanza three,
line three. Both Barlow and Dwight change Watts' original line,
"Satan the fowler, who betrays," but Worcester prefers Watts.

In numerous places, however, Worcester does adopt the changes
others had made in Watts, and in the vast majority of those cases, he
utilizes Barlow. The revisions of Psalms 100, stanza two, 47 CM,
77, 115 PM, 118 CM, 145 LM, and part of 147 LM second part all
belong to an uncredited Barlow.[37] In Psalm 41, Worcester retains
the "bowels" language in the first stanza, but prefers the Barlow
rendering of stanza two, line four, which rejects Watts' characteriza-
tion of God having bowels in favor of the word "mercy." Where
Barlow and Dwight disagree on a change, as in Psalm 47 CM, stanza
six, line one, Worcester chooses the Barlow revision.

On only one occasion does a Dwight or Mycall revision appear.[38]
Psalm 67 Worcester puts together as a pastiche of Mycall, Barlow,
and Dwight. Stanza one is Dwight's revision, stanza two, line one,
is Mycall's, and stanza four, lines one, three, and four, are Barlow's.
The rest is Watts.

1. Shine on our land, Jehovah, shine,
   With beams of heavenly grace;
   Reveal thy power through all our coasts,
   And shew thy smiling face.

2. Amidst our States, exalted high,
   Do thou, our glory, stand;
   And, like a wall of guardian fire,
   Surround the fav'rite land.

---

37. In the preface to the book, Worcester does note that some "amend-
ments" were made, but does not mention Barlow (or Mycall or Dwight for
that matter). Worcester, *Psalms, Hymns*, 3. This was not unusual for the
times, and for Worcester to imply that the work was Watts' would increase
its respect among potential buyers.

38. Actually, the revision in Psalm 118 CM, first part stanza one, line
three, is the same in both Mycall and Barlow. It is impossible to know
where Worcester took it from.

4. Sing to the Lord, ye distant lands,
   Sing loud with solemn voice;
   Let every tongue exalt his praise,
   And every heart rejoice.[39]

Clearly, then, twelve years after Dwight's supposed "replacement" for Barlow appeared, Barlow's work remained respected by publishers and paraphrasers and therefore continued to be sung in churches. Since no authors' names were attached to Worcester's revisions, however, the vast bulk of the people who sang the Psalms would not have known whose work they were and would have assumed probably that it was Watts. Worcester's Psalter was widely used in New England and beyond; Benson describes it as "one of the best recognized channels of Watts' ascendency over Church Song."[40]

The same is true for Lowell Mason and David Greene's 1831 *Church Psalmody*, which the Wellesley Congregational Church adopted in 1833 and the First Evangelical Congregational Church of Cambridgeport, Massachusetts, adopted in 1876 (superseding Worcester).[41] The preface to the work notes that it includes 421 metrical Psalms from Watts and that the authors modified and altered as they saw fit.[42] No mention is made of the use of others' alterations. While many of Barlow's changes are ignored,[43] fourteen Psalms appear just as Barlow had printed them in 1785.[44] In addition, two of the new versions of the Psalms omitted by Watts show up in Barlow's poetry, Psalms 108 CM and 137. Dwight's versions of 28 and 137 ("I love thy kingdom") appear, as do renderings of 137 and 140 which are not Barlow or Dwight.

Church Psalmody proved popular with many New England churches, and the Pastoral Association of Massachusetts approved its use in Congregational churches in that state.[45] Benson records that another Psalter popular among New England Congregational-

---

39. Worcester, *The Psalms, Hymns, and Spiritual Songs*, 150.
40. Benson, *English Hymn*, 168.
41. Chandler, *Wellesley*, 8; James S. Hoyt *The First Evangelical Congregational Church* (Cambridge: Harvard University Press, 1878), 71. Lowell Mason and David Greene, *Church Psalmody: A Collection of Psalms and Hymns adapted to Public Worship* (Boston: Perkins and Marvin, 1831).
42. Mason and Greene, *Psalmody*, viii.
43. For example, Psalm 73, stanza two, line two, remains in Mason as Watts, ignoring the Barlow revision. Mason and Greene, *Psalmody*, 140.
44. Psalms 21, 30, 47, 48, 60, 67, 72, 77, 86, 97, 100, 108, 125, 144.
45. Benson, *English Hymn*, 389.

ists was Hastings and Patton's 1836 *The Christian Psalmist*.[46] First Church Hartford, Connecticut, adopted this Psalter in the year of its publication to supercede Dwight's Watts.[47] The preface to this book explains that "the various readings have been compared with an original English copy containing his [Watts] own notes and observations."[48] The authors do provide names after the non-Watts Psalm versions they chose, although not after those that are mostly Watts' with revisions. After comparing those "various readings," the authors proceeded to include a goodly dose of both Barlow and Dwight in their final version. Sixteen texts contain Barlow revisions;[49] one text (Psalm 21, second part) contains Dwight changes.

The versions chosen of the Psalms Watts omitted represent both Barlow and Dwight, but curiously most of Barlow's are credited as "anonymous." The one exception to that is for his famous rendition of Psalm 137, "Along the banks where Babel's current flows." The new Dwight Psalms are all identified as his.[50] Did the editors not know who wrote the other Barlow pieces, or was Barlow's reputation still questionable even in 1836?

Apparently among the official ecclesiastical powers of Connecticut, Barlow's revisions continued to be suspect, for whatever reason. *Psalms and Hymns for Christian Use and Worship* in 1845 went against the grain of the more recent Psalters and chose to lift up many of Dwight's changes as definitive for practice.[51] This Psalter often solves the problem of archaic language or Britishisms simply by leaving out offending verses, as in Psalm 71 CM, second part. Barlow had made an aesthetic change in stanza six, line four, while Dwight had maintained the Watts stanza. This 1845 Psalter merely deleted the verse.[52] When they do utilize revisions of Watts, seven-

---

46. Thomas Hastings and William Patton, *The Christian Psalmist* (New York: Ezra Collier, 1836).

47. Walker, *Hartford*, 394. Curiously, it appears from Walker's text that these two were used side by side until 1845.

48. Hastings and Patton, *Psalmist*, 3.

49. Psalms 21, third part; 30, first part LM; 41; 48 SM, second part; 67 CM, first part; 72 LM, second part; 77 CM, first part; 86 CM; 97 CM, fourth part; 100 LM, second part; 107 LM, first part; 107 LM, third part; 107 CM, fourth part; 125 CM, first part; 127 LM, first part; and 129 CM.

50. Barlow's compositions included are Psalms 43, 52 (revised), 59, 60 (though revised in later verses), 108. Dwight's compositions included are Psalms 28, 54, 59, three versions of 88 (slightly altered), two versions of 140, 137 ("I love thy kingdom") and his "Proper Meter" version of 150.

51. *Psalms and Hymns for Christian Use and Worship*, General Association of Connecticut (New Haven: Durrie and Peck, 1845).

52. Ibid., 136.

teen Psalms appear with Dwight's changes as opposed to seven with Barlow's.[53]

Certain trends in the use of some revisions had begun to materialize in tunebooks and Psalters. For example, as noted above, Psalm 107 CM often appeared with Barlow's revision of the first verse. *Psalms and Hymns*, however, preserves Watts' original. On the other hand, Psalm 100 LM, second part, now commonly appeared with the Barlow change from

1. Sing to the Lord with joyful voice;
   Let every land his name adore;
   The British isles shall send the noise
   Across the ocean to the shore.

to

1. Before Jehovah's awful throne,
   Ye nations bow with sacred joy
   Know that the Lord is God alone;
   He can create and he destroy.[54]

Psalms and Hymns agrees with Barlow's change and implements it here.

Dwight also has the lion's share of the newly composed Psalm paraphrases here, although Barlow remains well represented (and uncredited). The editors did delete some of the stanzas of Dwight's Psalms, many of which were quite long, as in Psalm 28 LM where they begin with Dwight's stanza seven.[55] Barlow's additions are remembered by Psalm 70, first part, Psalm 75 (altered, and one of the few cases where a companion piece by Dwight does *not* appear), Psalm 88, first part, Psalm 108 CM, and Psalm 137.

Of these four Psalters common to New England churches in the first half of the nineteenth century, then, the only one to give

---

53. Dwight revisions are included in Psalms 21 CM; 37 CM, second part; 46 LM, first part; 47 CM; 58; 67 CM, first part; 91 LM, second part; 97, second part; 110 CM; 118 CM, first part; 125 CM, first part; 135 CM, first part; 139 LM, first part; 142 CM, first part; 145 LM; 147 LM, fourth part. Barlow's revisions are included in Psalms 4 LM; 19 SM, first part; 35 CM, second part; 75; 83; 100 LM, second part; and 112 CM.

54. Lines three and four here come from Watts' stanza two, lines three and four. Barlow dropped the first two lines of that stanza.

55. *Psalms and Hymns*, 59. Dwight's other Psalm paraphrases included are Psalms 54, 59 (two versions), 64 (two versions), 65, 70 (altered), 79 (altered), 88 (three versions, altered), 108 (altered), 137 (two versions) and his "Proper" Meter addition of Psalm 150.

Dwight precedence over Barlow was produced by the same organization that declared Barlow's original Psalter unfit for use in its churches: the General Association of Connecticut. Is it possible that, over thirty years after Barlow's death, the divines of Connecticut still felt his name to be unmentionable, even if some of his poetry was serviceable? Or could it be that Ezra Stiles' opinion that Barlow had tampered too much still held sway in Connecticut?

Although the Psalters noted above constituted the text for singing in public worship for the largest numbers of Congregational Churches in New England after 1850, the impact of Watts' American revisers was not limited to them. The worship of those churches of Baptist, Dutch Reformed, and Presbyterian traditions is not the subject of this study; nevertheless, a cursory glance at some of the Psalters in use in these traditions contributes to an understanding of the lasting influence of the changes in liturgical language wrought by Mycall, Barlow, and Dwight. Some of the revisions they made to Watts' Psalms (which were favorites in these other traditions as well as among the Congregationalists) spread from New England Congregationalism into neighboring Baptist churches and Dutch Reformed and Presbyterian churches in the Middle Atlantic States.

In his 1903 catalogue of the American revisions of Watts, Louis Benson makes careful note of the "Presbyterian editions" of Barlow's Watts.[56] The Synod of New York and Philadelphia voted in 1787 to allow the use of Barlow's revision of Watts to "be sung in the churches and families under their care."[57] A whole series of editions of Barlow's Watts followed under the specific title *Psalms Carefully Suited to the Christian Worship in the United States of America*. Benson's research uncovered these specifically Presbyterian versions printed until 1813, but he notes that books with that title, though without any notice of authorization included, appear until 1838.[58] As late as 1846, O. E. Daggett adds a footnote to his article on the Psalms, which indicates Presbyterians still using Barlow's revisions:

> We observe that a Presbyterian Assembly, which has been jealous of New England innovations, has yet retained in the last collection of Psalms put forth under its sanction, many or most of Barlow's alterations, which were long since eschewed in the region where they originated.[59]

---

56. Louis F. Benson, "The American Revisions of Watts's 'Psalms'," *Journal of the Presbyterian Historical Society*, II (1903–1904): 26ff.

57. Cited in Benson, "American Revisions," 27.

58. Ibid., 32.

59. O. E. Daggett, "The Psalms in Worship," *The New Englander*, July 1846: 327.

Daggett may have been referring to *Psalms and Hymns adapted to the Public Worship of the Presbyterian Church*, which was first published in 1835.[60] This volume contains almost every Barlow change. In addition, it includes seven of Dwight's added Psalms (70, three of Psalm 88, 108, and two of 137, including "I Love Thy Kingdom"). With a very few exceptions, it is Barlow's Watts, slightly revised and supplemented.

At about the time Daggett wrote, the Presbyterians brought out a new "official" Psalter, *The Church Psalmist*.[61] While still including numerous Barlow changes, the editors also brought back the original Watts in a number of places and borrowed some from Dwight's revisions as well.[62] The versions of Psalms omitted by Watts include representations from both Dwight and Barlow as well as other unidentified authors (none of the authors of Psalm paraphrases are identified in either Presbyterian book, though hymn writers' names are included). Thus well into the middle of the nineteenth century both Barlow's and Dwight's texts continued to be sung among Presbyterians.

One of the most popular books of Psalms and hymns among Baptists in New England (many of whom had originally been Congregationalists), the Middle Atlantic States, and the expanding frontier originally came from England: John Rippon's *Selection of Hymns*, meant as an appendix to Watts' *Psalms and Hymns*.[63] Samuel Holyoke's popular tunebook, *The Christian Harmonist*, noted above, was compiled as a musical companion to Rippon's collection, indicating that Rippon was also used in New England.[64] The most

---

60. *Psalms and Hymns adapted to the Public Worship of the Presbyterian Church* (Philadelphia: J. Whetham, 1835). This was officially approved by the General Assembly of the Presbyterian Church in the United States of America.

61. *The Church Psalmist* (Philadelphia: Presbyterian Publication Committee, 1847). The official approval for the volume seems to have been given in 1843.

62. For example, Psalm 53 CM ignores Barlow's revisions and returns to Watts; Ibid., 101. Psalm 46 LM, first part uses Dwight's alteration instead of Barlow's; Ibid., 89.

63. The first edition of this appeared in England in 1787 as *A Selection of Hymns from the best authors, intended to be an Appendix to Dr. Watts's Psalms and Hymns* (London: T. Wilkins). In 1820 a Philadelphia edition was first produced. For the purpose of this study, the following edition was consulted, *The Psalms and Hymns of Dr. Watts, Arranged by Dr. Rippon; with Dr. Rippon's Selection* (Philadelphia: David Clark, 1839).

64. Benson, *The English Hymn*, 204, note 141. The diary of a Congregational Church pastor, William Bentley of Salem, Massachusetts, mentions Holyoke's music more than once, implying that the tunebook, and perhaps

common form of Rippon used in New England Baptist churches
was compiled by James Winchell of First Church in Boston. "Winchell's Watts" was used so widely in New England Baptist churches
that an 1865 commentator described its popularity as "universal."[65]

By and large, the American version of Rippon stays quite close to
Watts' originals, generally making changes only in the cases where
Watts refers directly to Britain. In these cases, Rippon follows Barlow's changes more than any other single source, although occasionally Rippon's American compilers substitute their own changes.
For example, in Psalm 19 SM, first part, Rippon records in stanza
four, line one, "Ye Christian lands, rejoice," as opposed to Watts'
"Ye British lands, rejoice."[66] This is Barlow's revision. Other Barlow
changes from British references appear in Rippon's Psalms 47, 67,
75, 96, 100, 115, 145, and 147. A couple of times Dwight's changes
do appear, as in Psalm 104 LM, stanza twelve, line one, where the
word "Britons" in Watts is replaced by the word "nations" in
Dwight and Rippon.[67]

Oddly enough, as in Worcester above, John Mycall makes an appearance in two Psalms that are combinations of several revisions.
Psalm 21 CM in Rippon uses changes from Dwight and Mycall
(stanzas three and four) as well as unrevised Watts. The version of
Psalm 67 appears here with the same combination of changes used
in the Worcester version with one exception. Instead of using the
Dwight version of stanza one, line one, Rippon's Watts uses a new
revision: "Shine, mighty God, on this our land."[68]

In keeping with Rippon's practice of using the American revisions only in reference to political language,[69] the Psalms newly
composed by Barlow and Dwight to complete the Psalter are not
included, not even in the selection of hymns.

Winchell's version of Rippon[70] varies just slightly from the standard American text. In his preface, Winchell explains that

---

Rippon, was used in Congregational churches as well; see *The Diary of
William Bentley, D.D.*, Vol. 3 (Gloucester, Mass.: Peter Smith, 1962), 54.

65. R. H. Neale, *Address at Two Hundredth Anniversary of First Baptist
Church* (Boston, 1865), 38.

66. Rippon, *Psalms and Hymns*, 436.

67. Ibid., 80.

68. Ibid., 618 and 606.

69. The only change that is from a word other than some cognate of
Britain occurs in the omission, common to Mycall, Barlow, and Dwight, of
stanza six from Psalm 18 CM, second part. This stanza discusses how God
pours blessings on kings, therefore it has decided political implications.
Ibid., 610.

70. James M. Winchell, *Arrangement of the Psalms Hymns and Spiritual
Songs of the Rev. Isaac Watts DD* (Boston: James Loring, 1818).

by a careful comparison of the best editions both European and American, not a few of the typographical errors, and other alterations which have been accumulating for years, have been corrected.[71]

In keeping with that intent, and following Rippon, Winchell also leaves out the added Psalms and any change not overtly political in nature, including at least one place where Rippon had allowed a change. Instead of taking Barlow's revision of Psalm 100 LM, second part, stanza one, Winchell prefers Watts' lines one and two, Dwight's line three, and a revised version of Dwight's line four. So while Rippon, along with many tunebooks and other Psalters, reads:

1. Before Jehovah's awful throne,
   Ye nations, bow with sacred joy:
   Know that the Lord is God alone;
   he can create, and he destroy[72]

Winchell's Watts reads:

1. Sing to the Lord with joyful voice;
   Let every land his name adore;
   Let earth, with one united voice,
   Resound his praise from every shore.[73]

Aside from a couple of other minor changes, Winchell's Watts essentially agrees with the standard American version of Rippon, using selectively parts of Mycall, Barlow, and Dwight for revisions of material in Watts considered politically suspect.

Unlike the Baptists, however, the Dutch Reformed opted to use a considerable number of changes in their particular version of "Watts and Select" with added hymns and Psalms.[74] Like the Presbyterians, the Dutch Reformed were concentrated in New York and the Middle Atlantic States. Unlike the Presbyterians, who preferred Barlow, the Dutch Reformed used both Barlow's and Dwight's changes, but with a decided preference for Dwight, aligning them with their Congregational colleagues in Connecticut. In fact, in a couple of instances, they prefer Dwight's change, while the 1845 Connecticut

---

71. Winchell, *Arrangement*, vi.

72. Rippon, *Psalms and Hymns*, 60.

73. Winchell, *Arrangement*, 84.

74. *The Psalms and Hymns of the Reformed Protestant Dutch Church in North America* (Philadelphia: Mentz and Rovoudt, 1847). An interesting feature of this book is that no authors' names are attached to the Psalms, yet the hymns do have an index naming their authors.

Psalter (which superseded Dwight's Watts) used Barlow.[75] They also
retain several of the "Proper Meter" Psalms Dwight added, which
do not appear at all elsewhere.

Unlike Rippon and imitators, the Psalms Watts omitted are included here, in versions by both Dwight and Barlow, but with
Dwight having the majority of selections. The Dutch Reformed collection actually omits the one Barlow addition that seemed most
popular in tunebooks and other Psalters: Psalm 137, "Along the
banks where Babel's current flows." Instead, all three of Dwight's
paraphrases of this Psalm appear with all of their many verses. One
is left to wonder whether Barlow's reputation concerned the Dutch
Reformed more than the Presbyterians, or whether Dwight's more
consistent faithfulness to Watts swung the pendulum in his direction?

From the above material, it remains difficult to draw definite con-
clusions about the use of the language changes made by Mycall,
Barlow, and Dwight in public worship in New England into the
nineteenth century. Although many of the Psalms which were originally changed for political language simply saw offending verses
dropped, a few changes survived, as in Barlow's Psalm 100 alteration. Certainly some of the aesthetic changes found wide usage, as
did several of the Psalms in original paraphrases by Barlow or
Dwight, especially Psalm 137. The subsequent record indicates that
as worship patterns evolved through the early and middle stages of
the nineteenth century, a number of the revisions of or additions to
Watts' Psalter stayed with the worshipers of New England and the
Middle Atlantic States.

The significance of these changes and their staying power will be
considered in conclusion.

---

75. See especially Psalms 19 SM, first part, and 35 CM second part,
Psalms and Hymns of the Reformed, 40 and 67.

Chapter Seven

A Living Liturgy

Between the time Watts' Psalter came to the shores of America and the time Timothy Dwight revised it in 1801, the "name, language and story"[1] of Congregational Churches in New England changed dramatically. As reviewed in chapters two and three, not only the geo-political reality of the American colonists altered, but so did their social, linguistic, theological, and ecclesiological realities. The American revisions of Watts illustrate that liturgical language functions in the midst of historical shifts in two distinctive ways: liturgical language reflects the life of a worshiping community and its world and the changes in them, and liturgical language (and those who mold it) seeks to shape how a community responds to change. The American revisions of Watts' Psalter participate in both of those functions of liturgical language, and therefore in the shaping of the world of the New England Congregational churches well into the nineteenth century.

Liturgical Language Reflects the Changing Life of a Worshiping Community and Its World

In considering how Jewish liturgies revealed the life of the American Jewish communities in the last two centuries, Lawrence Hoffman observes:

> The utilization of a distinctive liturgical rite is simply one of the ways participating members of a group give public assent to their status as a community. . . . Borrowed from the past, it is an amalgam of the past and the present, a true representation of the worshipers themselves.[2]

---

1. Amos Wilder, "Story and Story World," *Interpretation*, 37 (1983): 361; see chapter one.

2. Lawrence Hoffman, *Beyond the Text* (Bloomington: Indiana University Press, 1987), 69.

The language of Mycall, Barlow, and Dwight woven into that of Watts told those who sang the Psalms into the nineteenth century as well as modern readers much about the community of the singers, an "amalgam of the past and present." The past was clear in the unchanged parts of Watts, the vast majority of the texts in any one Psalter. The past was also clear in the themes that the revisers picked up in their revisions and new texts.

The language of worship reminded the singers of their roots in both the Biblical past and their specifically Puritan past first, before bringing them into the present. That Puritan past went beyond New England, to the Calvinist roots of the centrality of scripture and, in worship, of metrical Psalms as mediated through Switzerland, the Netherlands, and Great Britain. The original source from which the revisers worked was deeply embedded in the English Calvinist heritage, for Isaac Watts' Psalter

> is suffused through and through with the spirit of the Independent meeting house, with its almost smug piety and hatred of the 'World,' its trials and persecutions, and its solemn joy in the ordinances of worship.[3]

As both Dwight and Barlow had sought to do in their epic poetry, they hoped in their Psalms to do what their Puritan ancestors had always done, that is, to use Scripture as "first and foremost the language of their community."[4] Surprisingly, Barlow may do this best in the Psalms he added to the collection. As opposed to the more free paraphrases of Dwight, Barlow stays very close to the Biblical Psalm in almost every case. He saw even fewer problems than Watts did in having his contemporaries sing of their own faith in the words of the Biblical Psalmists. Barlow's famous version of Psalm 137 illustrates this very well. While Dwight goes on at great length in three paraphrases (one of which doesn't even mention Babylon), Barlow stays very close to the English version of the Psalm with which he was acquainted. He assumed, perhaps, that those who sang these Psalms did not need intentional ties to modern situations in order for the words to make sense; Biblical language was still, in 1785, the language of Congregational worshipers, who could make the translation to modern life themselves, even as their ancestors had done.

---

3. Harry Escott, *Isaac Watts Hymnographer* (London: Independent Press, 1962), 154.

4. Joseph Bassett, "The New England Way and Vatican II," *The Unitarian Universalist Christian* 361 (1981): 59.

Both Barlow and Dwight use one image repeatedly that strongly ties their community to its Puritan past: the use of "Zion" or some other name for the nation of Israel as a substitution for Watts' use of British imagery or in their new Psalms. The millennialism of their ancestors comes through in this imagery, though exactly what is identified with Zion may change from Barlow to Dwight, as the next section indicates.

All three revisers, and those who followed them, strongly tie the community to the present realities of life as well. The most obvious way these three writers use language to reflect their community's status and the changes occurring in it is in their choice of words to replace Watts' Britishisms. The passage of time from Mycall in the midst of revolution to Dwight, twenty years away from it, shows clearly in the words they opt to substitute for Watts'. Mycall takes care to have the United States as a nation represented in the church's song, and to have the church identify itself as part of the new nation, under God. Repeatedly he uses words like "America" (Psalm 19 SM, first part), "our States" (Psalm 21 CM), "Columbia" (Psalm 115 and 147 LM, second part), and even specifically "New England" (Psalms 60 CM and 135 CM) to make clear the identity of the singers in as parochial a way as Watts had in Great Britain.

Even a few years later, Barlow, while still using some specific references to his country, does not feel the need to be as parochial or direct in establishing identity. Rarely does Barlow refer directly to the United States, but he makes clear in other contexts the identity of the singers' nation. For example, Barlow's version of Psalm 21 departs entirely from Watts, with the subtitle "National Blessings acknowledged." Stanzas three and four make what can only be a direct reference to the American revolution:

3. In deep distress our injured land
   Implored thy power to save;
   For life we prayed; thy bounteous hand
   The timely blessing gave.

4. Thy mighty arm, eternal Power,
   Opposed their deadly aim,
   In mercy swept them from our shore,
   And spread their sails with shame.

Though hardly subtle, this sort of particular allusion is rarer in Barlow than it was in Mycall.

By the time Dwight compiled his Watts, the United States had a Constitution and settled form of government. The lack of specific national references in Dwight reflects the more settled identity of the nation, and the fact that Dwight more often moves from a national allusion to refer directly to the *church* indicates that for Dwight the church's identity was of greater concern, and how the church might impact the nation's identity. In his 1816 "Observations on Language," Dwight commented on the importance of a nation establishing its identity through its language. He makes clear he is not interested in names and titles, but rather in the moral fiber of a people. He writes:

> It is a primary principle in all researches concerning language, *that nations will uniformly have such words as express those ideas which they wish to communicate.* . . . The character of a nation may with absolute certainty be extensively known from this source.[5]

What Dwight shows more than anything else about the situation of his time is that some conflict existed over what the "character" of this new nation was to be, as well as some conflict over the character of the church and its place in the nation. For example, in Dwight's version of Psalm 21, which Barlow used to refer to the revolutionary war, the main topic is the nation's rulers (Watts' subject had been the King). Dwight's stanzas three and four read as follows:

3. Then let them [the rulers] still on God rely,
   For wisdom and for grace;
   His mercy shall their wants supply,
   And save our happy race.

4. But, righteous Lord, thy stubborn foes
   Shall quake through all their bands;
   Thy vengeful arm shall find out those,
   That hate thy mild commands.

Perhaps the most obvious observation to make is that the singers of these Psalms would have noticed the changes in language and either seen their identity in them or rejected them. As numerous diarists of the time have indicated (see the quote from Joseph Buckingham on page 19), the New Englanders of the late eighteenth century knew their Watts, many of them having memorized his Psalm "imitations" from use in daily devotions as well as in public worship. Tunes in use were limited enough, even with the changes

---

5. Timothy Dwight, "Observations on Language," *Memoirs of the Connecticut Academy of Arts and Sciences*, Vol. 1, Part 4 (New Haven: Oliver Steele, 1816), 365. Italics in original.

brought by the singing schools, that people paid attention to the words in a way different from modern churchgoers. The Psalms were the words of daily prayer, and undoubtedly one of the reasons why local church histories indicate a slowness to change which Psalter they used is that people felt an emotional attachment to one or another version of this book of song and prayer, much as modern Christians express concern at a change from one Bible translation to another. The changes would have been noticed and either embraced as appropriately "identifying for the worshiper what it is that he or she stands for, what real life is like, what his or her aspirations are,"[6] or been dropped over time as irrelevant, something anathema to Puritan-inspired worship. The evidence, as noted in chapter six, indicates that many of the changes were kept in place even half a century or more after they were made. Obviously the churches and singers found their past and present reality revealed in the texts, or the texts would have dropped out of use. As Bruce Kuklick writes, "the church stood between the demands of faith and the realities of the world."[7] Mediating that distance "between" was the language of worship, and specifically, of these Psalms.

Liturgical Language Seeks to Shape
How a Community Responds to Change

The poet and Connecticut Wit John Trumbull understood that Barlow and Dwight were both seeking to shape the very language of the new country forming around them. He wrote these "Lines addressed to messrs Dwight and Barlow" in response to British criticisms of their attempt to shape the new American poetic language:

> Yet heed not these, but join the sons of song,
> And scorn the censures of the envious throng;
> Prove to the world, in these new-dawning skies,
> What genius kindles and what arts arise;
> What fav'ring Muses lent their willing aid,
> As gay through Pindus' flowery paths you stray'd
> While in your strains the purest morals flow'd,
> Rules to the great, and lessons to the good.

---

6. Hoffman, *Beyond the Text*, 69.
7. Bruce Kuklick, *Churchmen and Philosophers* (New Haven: Yale University Press, 1985), 9.

All Virtue's friends are yours. Disclose the lays;
Your country's heroes claim the debt of praise;
Fame shall assent, and future years admire
Barlow's strong flight, and Dwight's Homeric fire.[8]

Both Barlow and Dwight believed that, in Dwight's words, "with every change in society, an alteration in their language will take place."[9] Both attempted to shape that alteration through their poetry. The two differed in that Barlow wrote verse with the aim of establishing a new American literary style and corpus. Dwight, on the other hand, wrote to influence not only the future of American letters, but the future of the American character, both inside and outside the church. Dwight's many prose works, including his newspaper articles, illustrate this goal, but so do the Psalms he both revised and created for the General Association of Connecticut and the New England churches. The Psalters of the two men exemplify Howard's comment that Barlow and Dwight differed significantly in their imaginative reaction to their age.[10] Barlow was not satisfied merely to eliminate questionable references to Great Britain in Watts, but to take the opportunity to explore and push the limits of the language itself in a new context. In the churches around him, American musicians worked to shape a new American musical idiom. Were the texts to be sung to the new music to be those of the first quarter of the century, or would they reflect the new realities *and* shape a new language to live in those realities? These must have been Barlow's, and his collaborators', questions.

Dwight also sought to use the language to shape change, but he was less concerned in the Psalter about literary change than moral, spiritual, and political change. While Barlow worked his whole life to move the intellectual realm of the United States to greater heights (for example, his proposed scheme late in life to establish a national university), Dwight became part of the movement to resist the new and become entrenched in the Standing Order. Though at times in his life he, too, seemed to be on the cutting edge (for example, his concern for co-educational schooling), his vision for the church exhibits a defensive posture. He wanted to keep the church at the center of life in the United States, as it had been in colonial New

---

8. John Trumbull, "Lines Addressed to Messrs. Dwight and Barlow," *The Poetical Works of John Trumbull* (Hartford: Samuel G. Goodrich, 1820), 108–109. The poem specifically refers to Barlow's *The Vision of Columbus* and Dwight's *The Conquest of Canaan.*

9. Dwight, *Observations*, 377.

10. Howard, *Connecticut Wits*, 347.

England, and the only way he thought that could be done was by codifying the status quo of the last half of the eighteenth century.

If, as Taft writes, liturgy is best understood "in motion,"[11] then perhaps Dwight's Watts can best be understood as seeking to control that motion and keep it to a minimum. It reveals a church trying to hold on, in the midst of tremendous upheaval in all the realms of its influence, by grasping the conservative principle: fortify the status quo as a bulwark against the weapons of change.

Dwight's revisions and the new Psalms illustrate this in several ways. First, his commission from the General Association makes it clear that he was encouraged in this sort of conservatism by the power structure of which he was a part. Barlow had changed too many things, opening a door to lose too much of the sacred past. Dwight was to stick as closely as possible to Watts, changing only the language that truly conflicted with the new American situation.[12] Obviously, Dwight the poet struggled with this limitation, as he did make changes beyond the scope of a Mycall who stuck closely to changing only Britishisms. He remained faithful to the charge to a considerable extent, however, maintaining things like the "bowels" language, which was already archaic, and the subtitle to Psalm 115 in which Dwight retains the reference to a British holiday: the Fifth of November, Guy Fawkes' Day.

It is in his new texts, however, that the conservative tendency of Dwight—and the Established Church—shows most clearly. On the one hand, Dwight composed several texts in what he called "Proper" meter intended to suit the new music American composers were producing for use in churches. This progressive move is balanced, or perhaps counteracted, by the texts themselves. Again and again these texts seek to uphold traditional values and the traditional power of the church vis-à-vis the political and social powers of the world. Psalm 75 provides one example of this theme. Watts' paraphrase was applied, according to the subtitle, to "the Glorious Revolution by King William or the Happy Accession of King George I to the Throne." The text speaks of God dethroning a tyrant and bringing just rule to the land. Mycall and Barlow retain

---

11. Robert Taft, *Beyond East and West: Problems in Liturgical Understanding* (Washington D.C.: Pastoral Press, 1984), 154.

12. The irony of this, of course, is that the hallowed ancestors of the Congregational Churches of New England found Watts and those who preceded him innappropriate innovators, while they held on to the "pure" scripture in the Bay Psalm Book. No one in Connecticut suggested a return to that, but instead to the one-time outrageous innovator, now sacred Psalmist, Isaac Watts.

much of the flavor of the Watts, but apply the Psalm to, as Mycall's subtitle indicates, "the glorious revolution in America, July 4th, 1776." While all three of these paraphrases indicate God's place as ultimate ruler, Dwight takes pains to make that even more clear in the context of a democracy. His version of Psalm 75 is titled "Government from God alone. A Psalm for a General Election." The bulk of the text is a lesson to those aspiring to rule on how they should act in office and on God's power to remove them should they not act correctly. Stanzas two, three, and five illustrate the theme:

> 2. While from thy hand our rulers take their power
>   Give them thy greatness humbly to adore,
>   With hearts sincere to hold a righteous sway,
>   Bid justice triumph, and the proud obey,
>   Defend the poor, debasing bribes disdain,
>   Avenge bold wrongs, nor wield the sword in vain.
>
> 3. While round all realms wide dissolution's rolled
>   Give them the pillars of the earth t'uphold,
>   The meek, the wise, the faithful and the just,
>   And tread the vile oppressor in the dust;
>   To seek thy name, to love thy kingdom Lord,
>   And spread through earth the victories of thy word.
>
> 5. Teach them, that greatness power and place are thine
>   Gifts from thy hand, bestowed for ends divine,
>   Rulers, thy Stewards, to mankind are given
>   To shower the good and build the cause of heaven;
>   From thee a rich reward the faithful know;
>   The faithless hasten to distinguished woe.

While Watts, Mycall, and Barlow content themselves with a few vague threats of God's vengeance on tyrants, Dwight gives rulers a morality lesson, stressing the point that they are to hold God and God's work as their highest aim.

The defensive posture of the church against the changes going on around them in the political and social realms also appears in Dwight's added "Proper" Meter version of Psalm 83. Watts' 83 (closely followed by Barlow) tells a vague story of a complaint against "persecutors." Dwight makes the complaint crystal clear in "A Prayer of the Church against her enemies," with stanza three making the case plain:

> 3. Whate'er ingenious mischief can devise,
>   Or the tongue utter, trained to arts and lies,
>   Or envy wish, or malice fell prepare

Or atheist hope, or bold blasphemer dare,
They wish, they hope, they form, they dare they try
And sound the trump to combat with the Sky.

The rest of the text calls on God to defeat these enemies in rather
graphic terms so that "from shore to shore thy word in triumph
run." Similar themes of holding fast to the church as a fortress in
the conflict with change appear in Dwight's renderings of Psalms
43, 52, 59, 70, 75, 79, 108, and 140. His LM second rendition of
Psalm 137 carries a particularly clear stanza on this matter.

> 1. Lord, in these dark and dismal days,
>   We mourn the hidings of thy face;
>   Proud enemies our path surround,
>   To level Zion with the ground.

> 2. Her songs, her worship, they deride,
>   And hiss thy word with tongues of pride,
>   And cry, t'insult our humble prayer,
>   "Where is your God, ye Christians, where?"

In stanza four of that Psalm, Dwight shows his hand even more
clearly, "To happier days our bosoms turn." Those happier days are
described in his more pastoral texts, like Psalms 43 or 65, which
pick up themes from his Greenfield Hill days and the poetry he
wrote about that place.

The rest who write about Timothy Dwight's literary corpus note
that by late in the eighteenth century his work began to focus on
"the preservation of the civilization he had idealized in *Greenfield
Hill*."[13] Stephen Berk describes Connecticut as

> the center of confrontation between latter day Puritans and demo-
> cratic insurgents. Out of this battle came an elaborate apology for the
> traditional faith and culture of New England. Its chief architect was
> Timothy Dwight. . . .[14]

If, indeed, this is true, then Dwight's Psalter represents another
tool to be used for these aims. Dwight sought to shape the response

---

13. Leon Howard, *The Connecticut Wits* (Chicago: University of Chicago Press, 1943), 237; see also Silverman, *Timothy Dwight* (New York:
Twayne, 1969), 57 which comments that after this time, Dwight narrowed
his focus from "Columbia" as an example to the world to "Connecticut"
as an example to the rest of the nation.

14. Stephen Berk, *Calvinism versus Democracy* (Hamden, Connecticut:
Archon Books, 1974), 5.

of worshipers to what he saw as rising infidelity, immorality, and diversity in the United States. He sought to help strengthen the power of the church in the lives of individuals and in the ruling of the democratic nation. Through a book designed to be used both in public worship and private devotion, Dwight and the powers of the church in Connecticut were saying to the people of New England that

> America's gift to the future was not restless change, for the sake of change, not mere revolution, but the possibility of stabilizing the ideal present, universalizing it in time and space.[15]

The "ideal present" included control over much of life by the church, as had been the case in the past. The words of Dwight in his version of Psalm 19 reflect this aim:

> 9. From each presumptuous way
> My wandering feet restrain;
> So shall my life be free
> From every fatal stain.
>   Oh make me see,
>   Thou God of grace,
>   My thoughts and ways
>   Approv'd by thee!

A good deal of "wandering" was going on as the people, the church, and the other institutions of the new republic adjusted to the post-revolutionary transformations of the nation. "Approval," which for an orthodox Congregationalist like Dwight could only mean sanction not just from Scripture but from the church, meant continuing church influence and control over the life of the people. What Dwight sought was congregations singing, and believing from the heart, in the face of what he saw as attacks on the faithful from all sides, the words of Psalm 137:

> 1. I love thy kingdom, Lord
> The house of thine abode,
> The church our blest Redeemer saved
> With his own precious blood.
>
> 2. I love thy Church, O God!
> Her walls before thee stand,
> Dear as the apple of thine eye,
> And graven on thy hand.

---

15. Richard Hathaway, *Sylvester Judd's New England* (University Park: Pennsylvania State University Press, 1981), 59.

4. If e'er my heart forget
   Her welfare, or her woe,
   Let every joy this heart forsake,
   And every grief o'erflow.

6. Beyond my highest joy
   I prize her heavenly ways,
   Her sweet communion, solemn vows,
   Her hymns of love and praise.

Postscript: Reflections on Contemporary Studies

In her book on ritual studies, Nancy Jay writes:

> Trying to understand the meaning of ritual is not an act of acquisition but a work of relating; the understanding is not an end point that can be reached so much as it is a movement of turning toward the social world of the ritual actors. Like women's work, it is never done, but not consequently invalid.[1]

"Turning toward the social world" of Mycall, Barlow, and Dwight assists in understanding their method of revising and adding to Watts, and how those revisions illustrate the character of their social world and what they hoped that character might become. Mycall was caught up in the fervor of creating a new nation; Barlow sought a new intellectual, philosophical, and artistic life for that nation; Dwight hoped to keep the nation from abandoning its anchors in the past. All three worked, as had Watts, within a liturgical tradition that strongly asserted that worship must be overtly relevant to the lives and times of the worshipers. Their goals, and the way they worked with a piece of the liturgy of their tradition to further them, were not confined to their time or geographical location, and thus continue to impact our understanding of the shaping and function of liturgy.

Robert Taft writes:

> History can free us from the temptation to absolutize past or present by opening up to us the changing patterns—and hence relativity—of much in our practice and doctrine.[2]

---

1. Nancy Jay, *Throughout Your Generations Forever* (Chicago: University of Chicago Press, 1992), 13.
2. Robert Taft, *Beyond East and West: Problems in Liturgical Understanding* (Washington D.C.: Pastoral Press, 1984), 163.

Indeed, I would argue that one cannot understand past or present liturgy without studying the changing patterns not only of the words, acts, objects, and silences of liturgy, but also of the "social world" in which that liturgy was and is enacted. This is, I believe, the one piece missing from Hoffman's methodology (presented in chapter one), though very much present in his work. He stresses looking at three pieces of a liturgy to understand it: content, structure, and choreography.[3] I would add a fourth category: context. Hoffman himself does so in his studies in the book, and states at one point that "the real factor making for ritual differentiation is social, not geographical, distance. Through the way a community prays, it defines who it is, whence it comes, and how it chooses to express its own individuality."[4] The character of the time, place, cultural, and political systems in which the shapers of liturgy live inevitably has a profound effect on how pieces of a liturgy change. As Hoffman's work points out, that seems to be true across traditions, in varying degrees, and is not limited to those like Calvinists who are overt about liturgy being related to the lives and times of the people.

Nicholas Woltersdorff seems to question this inevitability when he writes:

> ritual gets established as a social practice; and it continues on its way amid many disputes over interpretation. Continuity is threatened, however, when one party succeeds in getting its interpretation expressed by words *within* the commemoration, rather than being content to let it remain in the background.[5]

Woltersdorff, I believe, is being disingenuous, for when has there been a time in history when liturgical change has not been influenced by the interpretations of those who shaped it? This practice certainly is not limited to Puritan worship, as one need only study the development of Eucharistic liturgies or the Reformation and Counter Reformation liturgical changes to see the obvious activity of interpretation of liturgy—and the impact of the social world in which that liturgy was being enacted—being expressed within the

---

3. Lawrence A. Hoffman, *Beyond the Text* (Bloomington: Indiana University Press, 1987), 69–72.

4. Ibid., 58.

5. Nicholas Woltersdorff, "The Remembrance of Things (Not) Past: Philosophical Reflections on Christian Liturgy," in *Christian Philosophy*, Thomas P. Flint, ed. (Notre Dame: University of Notre Dame Press, 1990), 141.

words and actions of the liturgy itself.[6] Hoffman's work makes this clear in modern Jewish liturgy as well.

Certainly the New England Congregationalists did not see their mode of liturgical change as threatening "continuity" with the faith of the past, but rather as uniting the continuous tradition with that of the present, an "amalgam" that gave life to worship. In Kuklick's phrase, they understood clearly their position "between the demands of faith and the realities of the world" as requiring that their prayers, songs, and sacraments in part provide that bridge "between."[7]

Of course, the dilemma pointed out particularly by the conflict between Barlow and Dwight, and by the rise in popularity of evangelical hymns instead of Psalms, is that liturgy most often is not shaped by the majority of the people who worship. Clearly, as the history of Watts' Psalter in America illustrates, the social, political, and cultural world inhabited and to some extent shaped by the worshipers impacts the liturgy, although, even in the Free Church tradition, liturgy, the "work of the people," is shaped by a small minority of professionals.

This process creates an inherent tension that must be recognized and explored in any assessment of liturgical change and development, and it relates to Woltersdorff's point about "continuity." Gail Ramshaw, in her work on sacred speech, unwittingly lifts up this tension perfectly. At one point in the book, she notes that "to be Christian liturgy, the sacred rhetoric is to be communal rhetoric."[8] Certainly for sacred rhetoric to be communal would seem to imply the participation of the community not only in its enactment, but in its creation. A responsive reading or unison Psalm would not a communal liturgy make, especially if the language is not appropriate to current vernacular (Ramshaw points out the change in meaning of the word "gay" in the last few years as an example). A few pages later, however, Ramshaw writes:

> Orthodoxy is written by that tradition of theologians who affirm the past and restate it. . . . Liturgy must express the consensus about orthodox faith, so that to pray these prayers is to be Christian.[9]

---

6. See, for example, how the words the Protestant Reformers used in their Eucharistic liturgies reflect their varying interpretations of Eucharistic theology. A helpful reference for this is Bard Thompson, *Liturgies of the Western Church* (Philadelphia: Fortress, 1961).

7. Bruce Kuklick, *Churchmen and Philosophers* (New Haven: Yale University Press, 1985), 9.

8. Gail Ramshaw, *Christ in Sacred Speech: The Meaning of Liturgical Language* (Philadelphia: Fortress, 1986), 16.

9. Ibid., 23.

Ramshaw begs the questions "Whose consensus and what orthodoxy?" Clearly the General Association of Connecticut felt that orthodoxy was compromised not so much by any word written by
Joel Barlow (for they continued to use some of his words into the
middle of the next century) but by his diversion in his lifestyle and
other writings from what they understood as orthodoxy both in
theology and in politics. Brian Wren, in his book *What Language
Shall I Borrow*, raises exactly the question that one must ask in any
discussion of liturgical changes: "Who benefits from . . . this or that
pattern of language and metaphor? What power and privilege (in
church and society) does God-talk help justify, legitimize and per-
petuate—or bring to light, question, and free us from?"[10] Wren goes
on to say that "Revelation is not disembodied, but incarnational"
for Christians.[11] The same is true of liturgy, and its creation, and the
incarnational aspect of the creation of liturgy must include a careful
consideration of who the people are who shape it and what their
agendas may be. Liturgical studies must pay attention to the lessons
learned in the past century of Biblical studies concerning the importance of the context of a piece of Scripture not only within the canon
itself, but within the social, political, and ecclesiastical setting in
which it was transmitted: by whom, for whom, and why in just
these words and structure.

Doing this in liturgy, as in Biblical studies, does not mean the
liturgy is any less a medium for God to speak to the people or the
people to speak to God, nor does it deny the validity of the continuous tradition. It simply helps, as Taft noted above, to "free us from
the temptation to absolutize past or present." As some of the rhetoric around the introduction of inclusive language has illustrated, it
is often all too easy to fall into the idolatry of liturgy, confusing
orthdoxy with the worship of words and acts created by human
beings, and using the threat of heresy to condemn that which threat-
ens the power base of a group of people rather than the faith itself.
This was certainly the case in Joel Barlow's treatment by the divines
of Connecticut.

The continuity of the liturgy expressing the continuity of the
Christian faith over the centuries obviously can be shaped in many
ways, as it was from the very beginning of Christian liturgical tradition.[12] In late eighteenth- and early nineteenth-century New En-

---

10. Brian Wren, *What Language Shall I Borrow?* (New York: Crossroad,
1989), 82.

11. Ibid., 101.

12. Much current discussion of liturgical and theological "orthodoxy"
presents a picture of the early church as speaking with one voice. Modern
liturgical scholarship, including such works as Paul Bradshaw's *The Search*

gland, people turned to the ancient words of the Psalms to help them make some sense of the dramatic changes going on in the world around them. They looked to the old words to help discern what the church and faithful Christians needed to be in the new world. They did not turn to sing the *same* words, however, as had their parents and grandparents. Rather they sought new interpretations altogether, as well as making changes in the old songs to fit new times. In the end, what made most sense in expressing the faith of the new Americans was not Timothy Dwight's vehement clinging to his version of orthodoxy nor even Joel Barlow's flights into his version of a new American poetic idiom, but rather new words altogether: the hymns of the Wesleys, of Watts, of the camp meeting, and of the evangelistic rally. These hymns were based in the Bible, but used new styles and idioms based very much in the experience of many people not always in the leadership of the churches.

Aidan Kavanagh writes that

> a liturgical act is a theological act of the most all-encompassing, integral, and foundational kind. It is both precipitator and result of that adjustment to the change wrought in the worshiping assembly by its regular encounter in faith with its divine source.[13]

It is also both precipitator and result of the adjustment to the change wrought in the worshiping assembly by its regular encounter in faith with its "social world." Thus is created a liturgy that is not just inward-looking, but is also capable of creating worlds both inside and outside the church. Those who create liturgies, and those who study them, must pay attention to both these encounters to be true to all the complexity of any liturgical act. For liturgy to be truly transformative—of the church, the world, and the individual worshiper—the language of liturgy must continue to reflect and to mold change in church and society, with sympathies toward continuity with the past and contemplation of the shape of the future. Mycall, Barlow, Dwight, and Watts each navigated this balance beam with varying successes. If liturgy, and the church's song that is part of it,

---

for the Origins of Christian Worship (New York: Oxford University Press, 1992), illustrate the diversity of early liturgical life, with each geographic and culturally distinct church center developing its unique styles in word and act. Only much later in the first millennium after Christ, through discussion and occasionally coercion and bloodshed, does Western liturgy and theology become more outwardly uniform.

13. Aidan Kavanagh, *On Liturgical Theology* (New York: Pueblo Publishing Company, 1984), 89.

is to be truly the "work of the people," it seems language within worship must continue to work on this balancing act.

"The people," if understood as encompassing those of the past, present, and future, and also those professionals who create and preside over the enactment of liturgy, and *also* the rest of the worshipers, provides the link that holds the tradition together and ensures that worship will continue to be living and lively into the next millennium and beyond.

Appendix One

Known editions of Mycall's, Barlow's and Dwight's revisions of *Psalms of David Imitated* 1781–1835[1]

The Mycall Revision

The Psalms of David, Imitated in the Language of the New Testament, and applied to the Christian State and Worship. By I. Watts D.D. The fortieth edition, corrected, and accommodated to the use of the Church of Christ in America. Newburyport: John Mycall, 1781.

[Same Title.] Boston: Peter Edes for J. Boyle, 1787.

[Same Title.] Boston: John W. Folsom, 1789.

The Psalms of David. Imitated, &c. Corrected and accommodated to the use of the Church of Christ in America. Brookfield, Massachusetts: E. Merriam & Co., 1802.

[Same Title.] Brookfield: E. Merriam & Co., n.d. [but said in the Brinley Catalogue to be of 1804.]

[Same Title.] Brookfield: E. Merriam & Co., 1812.

The Barlow Revision

1. Connecticut and Miscellaneous Editions
Doctor Watts's Imitation of the Psalms of David, corrected and en-

---

1. Based on Louis F. Benson, "The American Revisions of Watts's 'Psalms,'" *Journal of the Presbyterian Historical Society*, II (1903–04): 18–34, 75–89, and a search of *National Index of American Imprints Through 1800*, Clifford K. Shipton and James E. Mooney, eds. (American Antiquarian Society, 1969) and *American Bibliography*, Ralph R. Shaw and Richard H. Shoemaker, eds., vols. 1801–1835 (New York: Scarecrow Press, 1958–1985). This is a partial listing as, without examination of each volume, it is difficult to tell by title which version of Watts any one volume might be.

larged. To which is added A Collection of Hymns; the whole applied to the State of the Christian Church in General. Hartford: Barlow and Babcock, 1785.

[Same Title.] Hartford: Hudson & Goodwin and Nathaniel Patten, 1786.

[Same Title.] Hartford: Nathaniel Patten, n.d. [1787].

[Same Title.] Hartford: Hudson & Goodwin and Nathaniel Patten, n.d. [1790].

[Same Title.] New York: Durell, 1790.

[Same Title.] Hartford: Hudson and Goodwin, 1791.

[Same Title.] Hartford: Nathaniel Patten, [1791].

[Same Title.] New York: Durell, 1791.

[Same Title.] New York: Durell, 1795.

[Same Title.] Glasgow: David Niven, 1786. [Benson notes that copies of this frequently turn up in the United States and assumes it was printed for importation to Connecticut.]

[Same Title.] Hartford: Hudson and Goodwin, 1801.

2. Presbyterian Editions[2]

Psalms, carefully suited to the Christian Worship in the United States of America. Being an Improvement of the Old Versions of the Psalms of David. Allowed, by the reverend Synod of New York and Philadelphia, to be used in churches and private families. Philadelphia: Francis Bailey, 1787.

[Same Title.] Philadelphia: W. Young and J. James, 1788.

[Same Title.] New Brunswick: Shelly Arnett, 1789.

[Same Title.] New York: Hodge, Allen & Campbell, 1790.

[Same Title.] Elizabeth-Town: Shepard Kollock, 1791.

[Same Title.] Philadelphia: Francis Bailey, 1792.

[Same Title.] New York: Berry and Rogers and John Reid, 1792.

[Same Title.] Philadelphia: H. & P. Rice, 1793.

[Same Title.] Philadelphia: R. Campbell, 1795.

[Same Title.] Philadelphia: Francis Bailey, 1795.

[Same Title.] Glasgow: J. & A. Duncan, 1795.

[Same Title.] Elizabeth-Town: Shepard Kollock, 1797.

[Same Title.] Wilmington: Brynberg, 1797.

[Same Title.] Philadelphia: Campbell, 1799.

[Same Title.] Philadelphia: R. Aitken, 1802.

---

2. Numerous editions of Barlow's Watts carried the imprimatur of the General Assembly of the Presbyterian Church, thus making it an "official" Presbyterian edition. Benson notes those which carry this imprimatur. It is possible that some of those in the next section do also, but that fact has not been recorded in my sources.

[Same Title.] New York: T. & J. Swords, 1802.

[Same Title.] New York: n.p., 1804.

[Same Title.] Hudson: Harry Croswell, 1805.

[Same Title.] Albany: Websters and Skinners, 1816.

Psalms, carefully suited, &c. Being Dr. Watts' Imitation of the Psalms of David, as improved by Mr. Barlow. Allowed by the Reverend Synod of New York and Philadelphia, to be sung in congregations and Families. Philadelphia: Robert Campbell, 1799.

[Same Title.] Philadelphia: John McCulloch, n.d. [1802]

Dr. Watts' Imitation of the Psalms of David, suited to the Christian Worship, in the United States; and allowed by the Synod of New-York and Philadelphia, to be used in all the churches. Philadelphia: William F. McLaughlin, 1805.

An Imitation of the Psalms of David: carefully suited to the Christian Worship: being an Improvement of the former versions of the Psalms. Allowed by the General Assembly of the Presbyterian Church in the United States to be used in churches and private families. Albany: Websters and Skinners, 1813.

An imitation of the psalms of David carefully suited to The Christian Worship; being an improvement of the former versions of the psalms allowed by the General assembly of the Presbyterian Church in the United States. Albany: Charles R. and George Webster, 1802.

The Psalms of David, imitated in the language of the New Testament, and applied to the Christian Use and Worship. By I. Watts, D.D. A new ed. Approved and allowed by the General assembly of the Presbyterian Church in the United States of America. Albany: Websters and Skinners, 1817. (This could be either Barlow or Dwight.)

3. *Psalms Carefully Suited . . .* but not known to be official Presbyterian versions.

Psalms, carefully suited to the Christian Worship in the United States of America. Being an Improvement of the Old Version of the Psalms of David. Philadelphia: W. Young, 1793.

[Same Title.] Philadelphia: W. Young, 1794.

[Same Title.] Philadelphia: W. Young, 1799.

[Same Title.] Harrisburg: John Wyeth, 1803.

[Same Title.] New York: T. & J. Swords, 1804.

[Same Title.] Philadelphia: Thomas Dobson, 1805.

[Same Title.] Hagerstown: Jacob D. Dietrick, 1806.

[Same Title.] New York: D. & G. Bruce, 1806.

[Same Title.] Philadelphia: W. W. Woodward, 1806.

[Same Title.] Troy, New York: Moffitt and Lyon, 1807.

[Same Title.] New York: [n.p.], 1808.
[Same Title.] Albany: E. & E. Hosford, 1809.
[Same Title.] New York: Evert Duyckinck and M. & W. Ward, 1809.
[Same Title.] Philadelphia: W. W. Woodward, 1809.
[Same Title.] New York: Williams and Whiting, 1810.
[Same Title.] New York: D. & G. Bruce, 1810.
[Same Title.] New Brunswick: Ambrose Walker, 1810.
[Same Title.] Brooklyn: Thomas Kirk, 1811.
[Same Title.] Albany: E. & E. Hosford, 1812.
[Same Title.] New York: T. & J. Swords, 1812.
[Same Title.] New York: George Long, 1812.
[Same Title.] Pittsburgh: S. Engles & Co., 1812.
[Same Title.] Philadelphia: J. Rakestraw, 1813.
[Same Title.] Wilmington: Porter, 1813.
[Same Title.] Philadelphia: W. W. Woodward, 1814.
[Same Title.] Hartwick: Todds, Clark and Crandal, 1814.
[Same Title.] New York: George Long, 1814.
[Same Title.] Rutland, Vermont: Fay and Davidson, 1814.
[Same Title.] Baltimore: J. Robinson, 1815.
[Same Title.] Albany: E. & E. Hosford, 1815.
[Same Title.] Philadelphia: W. W. Woodward, 1816.
[Same Title.] New York: George Long, 1816.
[Same Title.] Paris, Kentucky: J. Lyle, 1816.
[Same Title.] Philadelphia: W. W. Woodward, 1817.
[Same Title.] New York: J. Seymour, 1817.
[Same Title.] Albany: E. & E. Hosford, 1818.
[Same Title.] New York: G. Long, 1818.
[Same Title.] New York: Samuel Campbell and son, 1818.
[Same Title.] New York: W. B. Gilley, 1818.
[Same Title.] Philadelphia: J. Rakestraw, 1818.
[Same Title.] Philadelphia: Woodward, 1818.
[Same Title.] Pittsburgh: Butler and Lambden, 1818.
[Same Title.] Wilmington: Robert Porter, 1818.
[Same Title.] Geneva, N.Y.: James Bogert, 1819.
[Same Title.] Philadelphia: Woodward, 1819.
[Same Title.] New York: W. B. Gilley, 1820.
[Same Title.] Philadelphia: Edwin T. Scott, 1821.
[Same Title, but "worship" misspelled as "worsihp."] Pittsburgh: Cramer and Spear, 1822.
[Same Title.] Pittsburgh: Patterson, 1822.
[Same Title.] New York: George Bruce, 1823.
[Same Title.] Philadelphia: Edwin T. Scott, 1823.
[Same Title.] Pittsburgh: R. Patterson & Lambdin, 1823.
[Same Title.] Pittsburgh: J. H. Lambdin, 1824.

[Same Title.] New York: George Bruce, 1826.
[Same Title.] New York: White, Gallaher & White, 1827.
[Same Title.] Philadelphia: Joseph Marot, 1828.
[Same Title.] New York: White, Gallaher & White, 1831.
[Same Title.] New York: Betts and Anstice, 1833.
Psalms carefully suited, &c. Being Dr. Watts's Imitation of the Psalms of David, as improved by Mr. Barlow. To this edition are added the words of sundry anthems. Wilmington: Peter Brynberg, 1805.
Psalms carefully suited, &c. Being Dr. Watts's Imitation of the Psalms of David, improved.. Wilmington: Robert Porter, 1818.
Psalms, carefully suited, &c. Being an improvement of the Old Version of the Psalms of David. By I. Watts, D.D.. Charleston, S.C.: William Riley, 1827.

4. The "corrected" Editions [Benson notes not much change from Barlow in these but the restoration of some Watts deleted by Barlow.]
Psalms carefully suited, &c. A new edition, corrected. New Brunswick: Lewis Deare, 1812.
[Same Title.] New York: Tiebout and Sons, 1817.
[Same Title.] New York: Daniel D. Smith, 1824.
[Same Title.] New York: John Montgomery, 1824.
[Same Title.] Princeton: D.A. Borrenstein, 1827.
[Same Title.] Same Printer, 1828.
[Same Title.] New York: Daniel D. Smith, 1830.
[Same Title.] Peekskill, N.Y.: S. Marks & Son, 1830.

The Dwight Revision

The Psalms of David, imitated in the language of the New Testament, and applied to the Christian use and worship. By I. Watts, D.D. A new edition, in which the Psalms, omitted by Dr. Watts, are versified, local passages are altered, and a number of Psalms are versified anew, in proper meters. Hartford: Hudson and Goodwin, 1801.
[Same Title.] Hartford: Sidney Press, 1803.
[Same Title.] Albany: Whiting, Backus & Whiting, 1804.
[Same Title.] New Haven: Sidney's Press, 1808.
[Same Title.] Hartford: Hudson and Goodwin, 1811.
[Same Title.] Same Printer, 1814.
[Same Title.] Montpelier, Vermont: Walton and Goss, 1814.
[Same Title.] Newburyport: W. B. Allen, 1814.

[Same Title.] New York: [n.p.], 1816.

[Same Title.] New Haven: S. Wadsworth, 1821.

[Same Title.] New York: Charles Starr, 1822.

[Same Title.] Rochester, N.Y.: E. Peck & Co., 1822.

[Same Title.] Hartford: Hudson and Goodwin, 1827.

[Same Title.] New Haven: N. Whiting, 1827.

[Same Title.] Philadelphia: L. B. Clarke, 1827.

[Same Title.] Hartford: P.B. Gleason and Co., 1830.

[Same Title.] New London: W. & J. Bolles and Collins and Hannay, 1830.

[Same Title.] New Haven: Durie & Peck, 1834.

[Same Title.] New London: Bolles, 1834.

[Same Title.] New York: Collins and Hannay, 1834.

The Psalms of David, . . . in proper meters. To the Psalms is added A Selection of Hymns. Approved and allowed by the General Assembly of the Presbyterian Church in the United States of America. Second Edition New Brunswick: A. Blauvelt, 1804.

[Same Title.] Albany: Websters and Skinners, 1817.

The Psalms of David, imitated in the language of the New Testament, and applied to the Christian Use and Worship. By I. Watts D. D. A new ed. At the request of the General Association of Connecticut. Hartford: George Goodwin and sons, 1817.

[Same Title.] New York: J. Seymour, 1817.

Psalms of David. Imitated in the language of the New Testament, and applied to the Christian State and worship. A new ed. by Timothy Dwight. Hartford: George Goodwin and sons, 1819.

Addendum to Appendix One

Recently Discovered Editions of Mycall, Barlow and Dwight

The Mycall Revision

The Psalms of David, Imitated in the Language of the New Testament, and applied to the Christian State and Worship. By I. Watts D.D. The fortieth edition, corrected, and accomodated to the use of the Church of Christ in America. Newburyport: John Mycall, 1792.

The Barlow Revision

Psalms, carefully suited to the Christian Worship in the United States of America. Being an Improvement of the Old Versions of the Psalms of David. Allowed by the reverend Synod of New York and Philadelphia, to be used in churches and private families. Philadelphia: John McCulloch, 1797.
[Same Title.] Newark: Benjamin Olds, 1832.

Psalms of David Imitated in the language of the New Testament and applied to the Christian State and Worship in the United States of America. By I. Watts D.D. Philadelphia: H. Adams, stereotyped by L. Johnson, 1828.
[Same Title.] Philadelphia: L. Johnson, 1830.

The Dwight Revision

The Psalms of David, imitated in the language of the New Testament and applied to the Christian Use and Worship. By I. Watts D.D. A new ed. At the request of the General Association of Connecticut. New York: John L. Tiffany, 1817.

Appendix Two

The Most Important Changes

The following pages set forth the most important changes Mycall, Barlow, and/or Dwight made to the Watts original. Many other differences exist, but most are grammatical or of less importance to the thesis of this study. The affected passages appear here in parallel columns, with Watts and Mycall on the left and Barlow and Dwight on the right. The Psalm number is denoted, along with its meter and any other signifying marks (i.e., first part, etc.). The specific stanza is indicated as "st3" and the lines of text as "l.2" or "ll.3&4." The Psalms Barlow and Dwight added, and several with more extensive changes, are included in appendix three.

A. Political Language

Psalm 19 SM First st4,l.1

<table>
<tr><td>WATTS</td><td>BARLOW</td></tr>
<tr><td>Ye British Lands rejoice</td><td>Ye Christian lands rejoice</td></tr>
<tr><td>MYCALL</td><td>DWIGHT</td></tr>
<tr><td>America rejoice</td><td>Ye Western lands rejoice</td></tr>
</table>

Psalm 47 CM st6,l.1

<table>
<tr><td>WATTS</td><td>BARLOW</td></tr>
<tr><td>The British Islands are the
    Lord's.</td><td>The Gentile nations are the
    Lord's.</td></tr>
<tr><td>MYCALL</td><td>DWIGHT</td></tr>
<tr><td>These ransom'd States are all the
    Lord's.</td><td>These Western climes are all the
    Lord's.</td></tr>
</table>

Psalm 67 CM st1,l.1

WATTS	BARLOW
Shine, mighty God, on Britain, shine.	Shine, mighty God, on Sion shine.

MYCALL	DWIGHT
Shine, mighty God, on all the land	Shine on our land, Jehovah shine.

Psalm 67 st2,ll.1&2

WATTS	BARLOW
Amidst our isle exalted high, Do thou our glory stand.	Amidst our realm exalted high Do thou our glory stand

MYCALL	DWIGHT
Amidst our States exalted high, Do thou our glory stand.	Here fix thy throne exalted high And here, our glory stand.

Psalm 67 st4,ll.1,3,4

WATTS	BARLOW
Sing to the Lord, ye distant lands While British tongues exalt his praise And British hearts rejoice.	Sing to the Lord, ye distant lands Let every tongue exalt his praise And every heart rejoice.

MYCALL	DWIGHT
Sing to the Lord, ye rescued States While thankful tongues exalt his praise And grateful hearts rejoice.	Sing to the Lord, ye distant lands Let thankful tongues exalt his praise And thankful hearts rejoice.

Psalm 67 st6,ll.1&3

WATTS	BARLOW
Earth shall obey her maker's will, Our God will crown his chosen isle.	Earth shall obey his high commands, Our God will crown his chosen land.

MYCALL	DWIGHT
Earth shall obey her maker's will, Our God will crown this chosen clime.	Earth shall confess her maker's hand, Our God will crown his chosen land.

Psalm 96 as 113 st2,l.3

WATTS
In Britain is Jehovah known.

BARLOW
But here Jehovah's name is known.

MYCALL
These deserts have Jehovah known.

DWIGHT
In these far climes Jehovah's known.

Psalm 97 CM st1,l.1

WATTS
Ye Islands of the Northern Sea.

BARLOW
Let earth, with every isle and sea.

MYCALL
as Watts

DWIGHT
Ye nations round the northern sea.

Psalm 100 LM st1

WATTS
Sing to the Lord with joyful voice;
Let every land his name adore;
The British isles shall send the noise
Across the ocean to the shore.

BARLOW
Before Jehovah's awful throne
Ye nations bow with sacred joy;
Know that the Lord is God alone;
He can create, and he destroy.
(lines 3–4 are from Watts stanza 2 lines 3–4)

MYCALL
Sing to the Lord with joyful voice
Let every land his name adore;
America shall send the noise
Across the ocean to the shore.

DWIGHT
Ye sons of men in God rejoice;
From land to land his name adore;
Let earth with one united voice,
Resound his praise from every shore.

Psalm 104 st12,l.1

WATTS
O bless his name, ye Britons, fed

BARLOW
His bounteous hands our table spread

MYCALL
O bless his name, ye nations fed

DWIGHT
O bless his name, ye nations! fed

Psalm 115 as 150 st6,ll.1&6

WATTS

O Britain, trust the Lord: thy
foes in vain,
And Britain blest the Lord that
built the skies.

MYCALL

Columbia trust the Lord; thy
foes in vain,
Columbia bless the God who
built the skies.

BARLOW

In God we trust; our impious
foes in vain,
And Zion bless the God that
built the skies.

DWIGHT

O Zion! trust the Lord; thy foes
in vain,
And saints adore the God, that
built the skies.

Psalm 135 CM st8,ll.1&3

WATTS

O Britain know the living God
He makes thy churches his
abode.

MYCALL

New England know thy living
God
He makes thy churches his
abode.

BARLOW

Ye nations know the living God
He makes the churches his
abode.

DWIGHT

O Zion, trust the living God
He makes thy courts his blest
abode.

Psalm 145 LM st4, l.3

WATTS

Let Britain round her shores
proclaim.

MYCALL

All nations round their shores
proclaim.

BARLOW

Let every realm with joy
proclaim.

DWIGHT

Let Sion in her courts proclaim.

Psalm 147 LM 2nd part subtitle

WATTS

A Song for Great Britain

MYCALL

A Song for America

BARLOW

no subtitle

DWIGHT

no subtitle

Psalm 147 st1,ll.1,3,4

WATTS

O Britain, praise thy mighty

BARLOW

Let Zion praise the mighty God,

God,
He bids the oceans round thee
flow;
Nor bars of brass could guard
thee so.

MYCALL
Columbia praise thy mighty
God,
He bids the oceans round thee
flow;
Nor bars of brass could guard
thee so.

For sweet the joy our songs to
praise
And glorious is the work of
praise.

DWIGHT
Bless, O Thou Western World,
thy God,
He bids the sea before thee flow;
Nor bars of brass could guard
thee so.

Psalm 147 st5, ll.1&4

WATTS
He bids the southern breezes
blow:
To call the Britons to his praise.

MYCALL
He bids the southern breezes
blow:
America! to draw thy praise.

BARLOW
He bids the warmer breezes
blow;
To call his people to his praise.

DWIGHT
He bids the southern breezes
blow;
To call thy children to his praise.

Psalm 147 st6, l.1

WATTS
To all the isle his laws are shown;

MYCALL
In all thy climes his laws are
shown;

BARLOW
Thro' all our realm his laws are
shown;

DWIGHT
To all thy sons his laws are
shown;

B. Theological Language

Psalm 2 SM st7

WATTS
He asks, and God bestows
A large inheritance
Far as the world's remotest ends
His kingdom shall advance.

BARLOW
Beneath his sovereign sway
The Gentile nations bend,
Far as the world's remotest
bounds
His kingdom shall extend.

MYCALL
same as Watts

Psalm 2 LM st9

WATTS
With humble love address the
    Son,
Lest he grow angry, and ye die:
His wrath will burn to worlds
    unknown,
If ye provoke his jealousy.

BARLOW
With humble love address the
    Son,
Lest he grow angry, and ye die:
His wrath will burn to worlds
    unknown,
His love gives life above the sky.

MYCALL
same as Watts

DWIGHT
same as Watts

Psalm 12 LM st1

WATTS
Lord, if thou dost not soon
    appear,
Virtue and truth will fly away;
A faithful man amongst us here
Will scarce be found if thou
    delay.

BARLOW
Almighty God appear and save!
For vice and vanity prevail;
The godly perish in the grave,
The just depart, the faithful fail.

MYCALL
same as Watts

DWIGHT
same as Watts

Psalm 16 CM first part st2

WATTS
Yet if my God prolong my
    breath,
The saints may profit by it;
The saints, the glory of the earth
The men of my delight.

BARLOW
Yet if my God prolong my
    breath,
The saints may still rejoice;
The saints, the glory of the earth
The people of my choice.

MYCALL
same as Watts

DWIGHT
Yet here thy children to sustain
Shall be my lov'd employ,
Thy children, first and best of
    men,
My friends, my highest joy.

Psalm 22 CM first part st7, l.3

WATTS
As Bulls of Bashan fierce and strong,

MYCALL
same as Watts

BARLOW
By foes encompass'd fierce and strong,

DWIGHT
same as Watts

Psalm 40 LM st3

WATTS
Lo! Thine eternal Son appears!
To thy desires he bows his ears;
Assumes a body well prepared,
And well performs a work so hard.

MYCALL
l.1 as Watts
l.2 To thy demands he bows his ears;
l.3 as Watts
l.4 as Watts

BARLOW
l.1 as Watts
l.2 To thy designs he bows his ears;
l.3 as Watts
l.4 as Watts

DWIGHT
In heaven, before his Father's throne,
Complacent, smiles th'eternal Son
And pleased, presents with boundless grace
Himself, a ransom for our race.

Psalm 48 second part st2, l.1

WATTS
With joy let Judah stand,

MYCALL
same as Watts

BARLOW
With joy thy people stand,

DWIGHT
same as Watts

Psalm 53 st4, ll. 3&4

WATTS
Jacob with all his tribes shall sing,
And Judah weep no more.

MYCALL
same as Watts

BARLOW
Thy joyful saints thy praise shall sing,
And Israel weep no more.

DWIGHT
same as Watts

Psalm 58 as 113 st1, l.3

WATTS
When th'injured poor before you stands,

BARLOW
When vile oppression wastes the land,

MYCALL   DWIGHT
same as Watts   When the oppressed before you
                                            stands.

Psalm 141 LM subtitle

WATTS   BARLOW
Watchfulness and Brotherly   Watchfulness and Brotherly
  Reproof   Love
MYCALL   DWIGHT
same as Watts   same as Watts

C. Miscellaneous

Psalm 6 CM st5, l.1

WATTS   BARLOW
He hears when dust and ashes   He hears his mourning children
  speak.   speak.
MYCALL   DWIGHT
same as Watts   same as Watts

Psalm 8 paraphrased st2, l.2

WATTS   BARLOW
A monument of honor raise   Their sounding notes of honor
                                              raise.

MYCALL   DWIGHT
same as Watts   same as Watts

Psalm 49 LM st4, ll. 2&4

WATTS   BARLOW
Laid in the grave for worms to   And leave his glories in the
  eat;   tomb;
And find th'oppressor at their   And hear th'oppressor's awful
  feet.   doom.
MYCALL   DWIGHT
same as Watts   same as Watts

Psalm 71 CM second part st6, l.4

WATTS   BARLOW
And drown'd them in his blood.   And saved me by his blood.

MYCALL
same as Watts

DWIGHT
same as Watts

Psalm 95 LM st4, ll.2&3

WATTS
Tempted their maker to his face;
A faithless, unbelieving brood,

BARLOW
l.2 as Mycall
l.3 as Watts

MYCALL
Yet tempt their maker to his
   face;
A faithless, unbelieving brood,

DWIGHT
l.2 as Watts
Provoked the vengeance of his
   rod.

Psalm 107 CM fourth part st1

WATTS
Thy works of glory, mighty
   Lord,
Thy wonders in the deeps,
The sons of courage shall
   record,
Who trade in floating ships.

BARLOW
Thy works of glory, mighty
   Lord,
That rule the boist'rous sea,
The sons of courage shall
   record,
Who tempt the dang'rous way.

MYCALL
l.1 as Watts
l.2 as Watts
l.3 as Watts
Where rolling ocean sleeps.

DWIGHT
ll.1-4 as Watts

Psalm 139 LM first part st4, ll.1&2

WATTS
Amazing knowledge, vast and
   great!
What large extent! What lofty
   height!

BARLOW
same as Watts

MYCALL
same as Watts

DWIGHT
How awful is thy searching eye!
Thy knowledge, O how deep!
   how high!

Appendix Three

Selected Psalms added by Barlow and Dwight or substantially changed from Watts

1. Psalm 21 CM All four different

   A. Watts version 1719
      "Our King is the care of Heaven."

      1. The King, O Lord, with songs of praise
         Shall in thy strength rejoice;
         And, blest with thy salvation, raise
         To heaven his cheerful voice.

      2. Thy sure defence through nations round
         Has spread his glorious name;
         And his successful actions crowned
         With majesty and fame.

      3. Then let the king on God alone
         For timely aid rely;
         His mercy shall support the throne,
         And all our wants supply.

      4. But, righteous Lord, his stubborn foes
         Shall feel thy dreadful hand;
         Thy vengeful arm shall find out those
         That hate his mild commands.

      5. When thou against them dost engage
         Thy just, but dreadful doom,
         Shall like a fiery oven's rage,
         Their hopes and them consume.

      6. Thus Lord, thy wondrous power declare,
         And thus exalt thy fame;

151

Whilst we glad songs of praise prepare
For thy almighty name.

B. Mycall "America the care of heaven."

1. Our States, O Lord, with songs of praise
    Shall in thy strength rejoice;
    And blest with thy salvation raise
    To heaven their cheerful voice.

2. Thy sure defence through nations round
    Has spread thy glorious name:
    And our successful actions crowned
    Thy majesty with fame.

3. Then let our States on God alone
    For timely aid rely!
    His mercy which adorns his throne,
    Shall all our wants supply.

4. But righteous Lord, thy stubborn foes
    Shall feel thy dreadful hand;
    Thy vengeful arm shall find out those
    Who hate thy mild command.

5. When thou against them dost engage
    Thy just, but dreadful, doom
    as Watts . . .

6. As Watts

C. Barlow "National Blessings acknowledged."

1. In thee great God, with songs of praise,
    Our favoured realms rejoice;
    And, blest with thy salvation, raise
    To heaven their cheerful voice.

2. Thy sure defence, through nations round,
    Hath spread our rising name,
    And all our feeble efforts crowned
    With freedom and with fame.

3. In deep distress our injured land
    Implored thy power to save;
    For life we prayed; thy bounteous hand
    The timely blessing gave.

4. Thy mighty arm, eternal Power,
    Opposed their deadly aim,
    In mercy swept them from our shore,
    And spread their sails with shame.

5. On thee, in want, in woe or pain,
   Our hearts alone rely;
   Our rights thy mercy will maintain,
   And all our wants supply.

6. Thus, Lord, thy wondrous power declare,
   And still exalt thy fame;
   While we glad songs of praise prepare,
   For thine Almighty name.

D. Dwight "Rulers are the care of heaven"

1. Our Rulers, Lord, with songs of praise
   Shall in thy strength rejoice,
   And blest with thy salvation, raise
   To heaven their cheerful voice.

2. Thy sure defence through nations round
   Has spread their honors far;
   And their successful measures crowned,
   Alike in peace and war.

3. Then let them still on God rely,
   For wisdom, and for grace;
   His mercy shall their wants supply,
   And save our happy race.

4. But, righteous Lord, thy stubborn foes
   Shall quake through all their bands;
   Thy vengeful arm shall find out those,
   That hate thy mild commands.

5 and 6 as Watts.

2. Psalm 28 LM Missing in Watts, Mycall.

A. Barlow: "God the Refuge of the Afflicted."

1. To thee, O Lord, I raise my cries:
   My fervent prayer in mercy hear;
   For ruin waits my trembling soul,
   If thou refuse a gracious ear.

2. When suppliant toward thy holy hill,
   I lift my mournful hands to pray,
   Afford thy grace, nor drive me still,
   With impious hypocrites away

3. To sons of falsehood, that despise
   The works and wonders of thy reign,

Thy vengeance gives the due reward,
And sinks their souls to endless pain.

4. But, ever blessed be the Lord,
Whose mercy hears my mournful voice,
My heart, that trusted in his word,
In his salvation shall rejoice.

5. Let every saint, in sore distress,
By faith approach his Saviour God;
Then grant, O Lord, thy pardoning grace,
And feed thy church with heavenly food.

B. Dwight: "Prayer and Praise to God for deliverance from temptations, and enemies."

1. O God of grace, my cry attend!
Lest, like the sons of guilt become,
Beguiled by Satan, I descend
With hopeless wretches to the tomb.

2. To thee my humble sighs arise;
My lifted hands wilt thou regard;
And let my penitence and cries
Find in thy house a rich reward.

3. O save my soul from shame and sin,
Nor let my heedless footsteps go
Where hardened wretches swift decline
Down the broad way to endless woe.

4. While peace their flattering lips proclaim,
And love profess, and hope impart,
They blast their neighbour's honest fame,
And wing their arrows to his heart.

5. But, while they plant the secret snare,
Thy searching eyes their path regard,
Thy hands their dreadful doom prepare,
And mete their guilt its just reward.

6. Because their hearts thy works despise,
Thy works of wisdom, grace, and power,
Thy hand, regardless of their cries,
Shall sink them, that they rise no more.
PAUSE

7. Blest be the Lord, who heard my prayer,
The Lord my shield, my help, my song,
Who saved my soul from sin and fear,
And tuned with praise my thankful tongue.

8. In the dark hour of deep distress,
   By foes beset, of death afraid,
   My spirit trusted in his grace,
   And sought, and found, his heavenly aid.

9. O blest Redeemer of mankind!
   Thy shield, thy saving strength, shall be
   The shield, the strength, of every mind,
   That loves his name, and trusts in thee.

10. Remember, Lord, thy chosen seed;
    Israel defend from guilt and woe;
    Thy flock in richest pastures feed,
    And guard their steps from every foe.

11. Zion exalt, her cause maintain,
    With peace and joy her courts surround,
    In showers let endless blessings rain,
    And Saints eternal praise resound.

3. Psalm 43: missing in Watts and Mycall.

   A. Barlow: CM "Safety in Divine Protection"

   1. Judge me, O God, and plead my cause,
      Against a sinful race;
      From vile oppression and deceit
      Secure me by thy grace.

   2. On thee my steadfast hope depends,
      And am I left to mourn?
      To sink in sorrows, and in vain,
      Implore thy kind return?

   3. O send thy light to guide my feet,
      And bid thy truth appear,
      Conduct me to thy holy hill,
      To taste thy mercies there.

   4. Then to thy altar, oh my God,
      My joyful feet shall rise,
      And my triumphant songs shall praise,
      The God that rules the skies.

   5. Sink not, my soul, beneath thy fear,
      Nor yield to weak despair;
      For I shall live to praise the Lord,
      And bless his guardian care.

   B. Dwight: Proper meter: "A complaint, mingled with hope, under great trials, particularly, long detention from public worship."

1. My God, defend my cause
   Against a host of foes;
   O save me from th'unjust,
   Who triumph in my woes!
      Why dost thou faint,
      My trembling heart?
      To God impart
      Thy sad complaint.

2. Why dost thou, O my shield,
   Desert me thus forlorn?
   Why, hated and oppressed,
   Thus bid me ceaseless mourn?
      To God I fly
      In God I'll trust,
      When low in dust
      My head shall lie.

3. Now to thy sacred house
   With joy direct my feet,
   Where saints with morning vows
   In full assembly meet.
      Thy power divine
      Shall there be shown,
      And from thy throne
      Thy mercy shine.

4. O send thy light abroad!
   Thy truth with heavenly ray
   Shall lead my soul to God,
   And guide my doubtful way;
      I'll hear thy word
      With faith sincere,
      And learn to fear
      And praise the Lord.

5. There reach thy bounteous hand,
   And all my sorrows heal;
   There health and strength divine
   Oh make my bosom feel!
      Like balmy dew,
      Shall Jesus' voice
      My bones rejoice,
      My strength renew.

6. Then in thy holy hill
   Before thine altar, Lord,

My harp and song shall sound
The glories of thy word.
  Henceforth to thee,
  O God of grace,
  A hymn of praise
  My life shall be.

7. My soul, awake to joy,
   And triumph in the Lord,
   My health, my hope, my song,
   And my divine reward.
     Ye fears remove;
     No more I mourn,
     But blest return
     To sing his love.

4. Psalm 52 LM Missing in Watts and Mycall

   A. Barlow: "The folly of self-dependence."

      1. Why should the haughty hero boast,
         His vengeful arm, his warlike host!
         While blood defiles his cruel hand,
         And desolation wastes the land.

      2. He joys to hear the captive's cry,
         The widow's groan, the orphan's sigh;
         And when the wearied sword would spare,
         His falsehood spreads the fatal snare.

      3. He triumphs in the deeds of wrong,
         And arms with rage his impious tongue;
         With pride proclaims his dreadful power,
         And bids the trembling world adore.

      4. But God beholds, and with a frown,
         Casts to the dust his honours down;
         The righteous freed, their hopes recall,
         And hail the proud oppressors fall.

      5. How low th'insulting tyrant lies,
         Who dared th'eternal power despise;
         And vainly deemed with envious joy,
         His arm almighty to destroy.

      6. We praise the Lord, who heard our cries,
         And sent salvation from the skies;
         The saints, who saw our mournful days,
         Shall join our grateful songs of praise.

B. Dwight: "The pride, folly and miserable end, of the Wicked: especially of Infidels."

1. Why do the wicked boast of sin,
   And steel their hearts against the Lord!
   His goodness shall forever shine;
   Forever stand his holy word.

2. Their thoughts all subtleties devise;
   Their tongues are edged like razors keen;
   Their fairest tales are flattering lies,
   By youth and innocence unseen.

3. Their hearts delight in guile and wrong,
   In truth perplexed and souls o'erthrown,
   Hence scorn and falsehood rule their tongue,
   And hence their feet to mischief run.

4. Thy law and gospel they despise,
   Vain of their taunts, of madness proud;
   Too rich thy grace to seek, or prize,
   To bow too lofty, even to God.

5. "From ancient days" with scoffs they cry,
   "All things their steadfast course maintain;
   "We see no God in earth, or sky,
   " And find his boasted promise vain."

6. Like raging fire thy wrath shall burn;
   Thy besom sweep them to the grave;
   Their branch, their root, thy hand o'erturn,
   And not a friend be found to save.

7. Their end the righteous shall behold,
   And say with an indignant smile,
   "These are the worshippers of gold,
   The sons of violence and guile."

8. "They placed their hopes in glittering dust,
   Chained to the earth, and glued to sin,
   But scorned to make the Lord their trust,
   Nor formed a wish for life divine."

9. Down to the grave the wretches go,
   By worms consumed, to ruin driven,
   Their spirits haste to endless woe,
   And find no entrance into heaven.

10. Then shall their joys revive no more
    Like dreams dissolved in fleeting air;

Their flatteries and their boasts be o'er,
And hopes all vanish in despair.

11. But in thy courts will I be seen,
    Growing in faith, and hope, and love,
    Like olives faith, and fresh, and green,
    And ripening for the world above.

12. There will I learn thy glory, Lord,
    And songs for all thy goodness raise;
    There will I wait to hear thy word,
    While listening saints approve the praise.

5. Psalm 53 Proper meter appears only in Dwight "The last verse paraphrased together with several passages from Isaiah, Malachi and St. Paul. Prayer for latter-day glory."

   1. Lord of all worlds, incline thy bounteous ear;
      Thy children's voice with tender mercy hear;
      Bear thy blest promise, fixed as hills, in mind,
      And shed renewing grace on lost mankind;
      Oh let thy Spirit like soft dews descend;
      Thy Gospel run to earth's remotest end!

   2. Let Zion's walls before thee ceaseless stand,
      Dear as thine eye, and graven on thy hand;
      From earth's far regions Jacob's sons restore,
      Oppressed by man, and scourged by thee, no more,
      Enriched with gold; adorned with heavenly grace,
      Truth their sole guide, and all their pleasure praise.

   3. Then Satan's kingdom shall from earth retire,
      Dead forms dissolve and furious zeal expire;
      The beast's fell throne shall darkness dire surround;
      Mohammed's empire crumble to the ground;
      The dreams of Infidels in smoke decay,
      And all the foes of heaven shall flee away.

   4. In barren wilds shall living waters spring;
      Fair temples rise, and songs of transport ring;
      The savage mind with sweet affections warm,
      And light and love, the yielding bosom charm;
      From sin's oblivious sleep the soul arise,
      And grace, and goodness, shower from balmy skies.

   5. Then shall mankind no more in darkness mourn;
      Then happy Nations in a day be born;
      From east to west thy glorious name be one,
      And one pure worship hail th'eternal Son;

Remotest realms one spotless faith unite,
And o'er all regions beam the Gospel's light.

6. Then shall thy saints exult with joy divine;
   Their virtues quicken, and their lives refine;
   Their souls improve, their songs more grateful rise,
   And sweeter incense cheer the morning skies;
   Heaven o'er the world unfold a brighter day,
   And Jesus spread his reign from sea to sea.

6. Psalm 54 is missing in Watts and Mycall.

   A. Barlow CM

       1. Behold us, Lord, and let our cry
          Before thy throne ascend,
          Cast thou on us a pitying eye,
          And still our lives defend.

       2. For slaughtering foes insult us round,
          Oppressive, proud and vain,
          They cast thy temples to the ground,
          And all our rites profane.

       3. Yet thy forgiving grace we trust,
          And in thy power rejoice;
          Thine arm shall crush our foes to dust,
          Thy praise inspire our voice.

       4. Be thou with those whose friendly hand
          Upheld us in distress,
          Extend thy truth through every land,
          And still thy people bless.

   B. Dwight Proper, as the 122nd: "Prayer for deliverance from
       enemies."

       1. My God, preserve my soul;
          Oh make my spirit whole!
          To save me let thy strength appear;
          Strangers my steps surround;
          Their pride and rage confound,
          And bring thy great salvation near.

       2. Those that against me rise
          Are Aliens from the skies;
          They have thy church and kingdom, Lord!
          They mock thy fearful name;
          They glory in their shame,
          Nor heed the wonders of thy word.

3. But O thou King divine,
   My chosen friends are thine,
   The men that still my soul sustain:
   Wilt thou my foes subdue,
   And form their hearts anew,
   And snatch them from eternal pain.

4. Escaped from every woe,
   Oh grant me, here below,
   To praise thy name, with those I love;
   And when beyond the skies
   Our souls unbodied rise,
   Unite us in the realms above.

7. Psalm 59 is missing in Watts and Mycall

   A. Barlow SM: "Prayer for national deliverance."

   1. From foes, that round us rise,
      O God of heaven, defend,
      Who brave the vengeance of the skies,
      And with thy saints contend.

   2. Behold, from distant shores,
      And desert wilds they come,
      Combine for blood their barbarous force,
      And through thy cities roam.

   3. Beneath the silent shade,
      Their secret plots they lay,
      Our peaceful walls by night invade,
      And waste the fields by day.

   4. And will the God of grace,
      Regardless of our pain,
      Permit secure that impious race,
      To riot in their reign?

   5. In vain their secret guile,
      Or open force they prove;
      His eye can pierce the deepest veil,
      His hand their strength remove.

   6. Yet save them, Lord, from death,
      Lest we forget their doom;
      But drive them with thine angry breath,
      Through distant lands to roam.

   7. Then shall our grateful voice
      Proclaim our guardian God;
      The nations round the earth rejoice,
      And sound the praise abroad.

B. Dwight Proper Meter "Together with some passages of the
    58th omitted by Doctor Watts. Complaints against
    Unbelievers."

1. Oh save thy Servants, Lord!
    Fulfill thy gracious word,
    For evil men against us rise;
    Causeless our souls they hate;
    Against our lives they wait,
    and aim their malice at the skies.

2. In sin their hearts delight;
    In sin their hands unite;
    Estranged and evil, from the womb;
    With lies their tongues begin;
    They grow in every sin,
    Till down they hasten to the tomb.

3. Deaf to that charming voice,
    That bids the world rejoice,
    The Gospel sound of pardoning love,
    The calls of gentle peace,
    The hopes of life and bliss,
    And glory, in the world above.

4. Blind to those truths divine,
    That, fair and lovely, shine,
    And teach the Godhead there alone,
    Tidings of peace refined,
    And joy to all mankind,
    And mercy to a world undone;

5. They hate thy glory, Lord,
    They mock thy holy word;
    The snares of death their hands employ;
    With flattery, and deceit
    For souls they lie in wait,
    And help the fowler to destroy.

C. Dwight Proper Meter Second Part: "Miserable end of the
    Wicked."

1. When God in wrath shall rise,
    T'avenge deceit and lies,
    What anguish shall the wicked tear,
    The men that slight thy name,
    That boast of sin and shame,
    And proudly cry, "What God shall hear?"

2. Thou hear'st, omniscient Lord,
   Each curse, and idle word,
   And all the scoffs of lips profane;
   And when the night of death
   Shall stop their impious breath,
   Their souls shall seek for peace in vain.

3. Then shall the Judge deride
   Their malice, and their pride,
   And crush them with an iron rod;
   In vain shall fall their tears;
   In vain ascend their prayers;
   And they shall know the ruling God.

4. Just as th'untimely birth
   Returns to moldering earth,
   Or streams in summer pass away,
   So all their dreams of peace,
   And promises of bliss,
   Shall vanish in that dreadful day.

5. O how will sinners need
   An Advocate to plead,
   Accepted at thine awful throne!
   How, in that solemn hour,
   Will faith's transcendent power
   Outweigh all things beneath the sun!

6. Yet save their souls, O Lord;
   Subdue them by thy word,
   Through all their powers oppose thy reign;
   As scattered foes submit,
   Bow them beneath thy feet,
   Nor let them read thy wrath in vain.

8. Psalm 60 CM

   A. Watts: "On a Day of Humiliation for Disappointments in War"

   1. Lord, hast thou cast the nation off?
      Must we forever mourn?
      Wilt thou indulge immortal wrath?
      Shall mercy never return?

   2. The terror of one frown of thine
      Melts all our strength away;
      Like men that totter, drunk with wine,
      We tremble in dismay.

    3. Great-Britain shakes beneath thy stroke,
       And dreads thy threatening hand;
       O heal the island thou has broke;
       Confirm the wavering land.

    4. Lift up a banner in the field
       For those that fear thy name;
       Save thy beloved with thy shield,
       And put our foes to shame.

    5. Go with our armies to the fight,
       Like a confederate God;
       In vain confederate powers unite
       Against thy lifted rod.

    6. Our troops shall gain a wide renown
       By thy assisting hand;
       Tis God that treads the mighty down,
       And makes the feeble stand.

B. Mycall subtitle as Watts

    1. Lord, hast thou cast New England off?
       Must we for ever mourn?
       Wilt thou indulge immortal wrath?
       Shall mercy ne'er return?

    2. As Watts

    3. New England shakes beneath thy stroke,
       And dreads thy threatening hand;
       O heal the people thou hast broke,
       Restore the trembling land.

    4,5,6 as Watts

C. Barlow: "Looking to God in the distress of war."

    1. Lord, thou has scourged our guilty land,
       Behold thy people mourn;
       Shall vengeance ever guide thy hand?
       And mercy ne'er return?

    2. Beneath the terrors of thine eye,
       Earth's haughty towers decay;
       Thy frowning mantle spreads the sky,
       And mortals melt away.

    3. Our Sion trembles at thy stroke,
       And dreads thy lifted hand!
       Oh, heal the people thou has broke,
       And save the sinking land.

4. Exalt thy banner in the field,
   For those that fear thy name;
   From barbarous hosts our nation shield,
   And put our foes to shame.

5. Attend our armies to the fight,
   And be their guardian God;
   In vain shall numerous powers unite,
   Against thy lifted rod.

6. Our troops, beneath thy guiding hand,
   Shall gain a glad renown:
   Tis God who makes the feeble stand,
   And treads the mighty down.

D. Dwight subtitle as Watts

   1,2 as Watts

   3. Thy people shake beneath thy stroke,
      And dread thy threatening hand;
      Oh heal the nation thou hast broke,
      Confirm the wavering land.

   4,5,6 as Watts.

9. Psalm 70 is missing in Watts and Mycall

   A. Barlow CM: "Protection against Personal Enemies."

      1. In haste, O God, attend my call,
         Nor hear my cries in vain;
         Oh let thy speed prevent my fall,
         And still my hope sustain.

      2. When foes insidious wound my name,
         And tempt my soul astray,
         Then let them fall with lasting shame,
         To their own plots a prey.

      3. While all that love thy name rejoice,
         And glory in thy word,
         In thy salvation raise their voice,
         And magnify the Lord.

      4. O thou my help in time of need,
         Behold my sore dismay;
         In pity hasten to my aid,
         Nor let thy grace delay.

   B. Dwight LM "Paraphrased together with several other passages of Scripture. A prayer of the Church for the Presence of Christ."

1. Oh thou, whose hand the kingdom sways,
   Whom earth, and hell and heaven obeys,
   To help thy chosen sons appear,
   And show thy power and glory here!

2. While stupid wretches, sunk in sleep,
   Slide onward to the fiery deep,
   To sense, and sin, and madness, given
   Believe no hell, and wish no heaven;

3. While fools deride, while foes oppress,
   And Zion mourns in deep distress;
   Her friends withdraw, her foes grow bold,
   Truth fails, and love is waxen cold;

4. Oh haste, with every gift inspired,
   With glory, truth, and grace, attired,
   Thou Star of heavens eternal morn;
   Thou Sun, whom beams divine adorn!

5. Assert the honor of thy name;
   O'erwhelm thy foes with fear and shame;
   Bid them beneath thy footstool lie,
   Nor let their souls forever die.

6. Saints shall be glad before thy face,
   And grow in love, and truth, and grace,
   Thy church shall blossom in thy sight,
   And fruits of peace, and pure delight.

7. Oh hither, then, thy footsteps bend;
   Swift as a roe, from hills descend;
   Mild as the sabbath's cheerful ray,
   Till life unfolds eternal day!

10. Psalm 75

   A. Watts: "Power and Government from God Alone. Applied
      to the glorious Revolution by King William, or the Happy
      Accession of King George I to the Throne."

      1. To thee most holy and most high,
         To thee we bring our thankful praise
         Thy works declare thy name is nigh,
         Thy works of wonder and of grace.

      2. Britain was doomed to be a slave,
         Her frame dissolved, her fears were great;
         When God a new supporter gave,
         To bear the pillars of the state.

3. He from thy hand received his crown,
   And swear to rule by wholesome laws;
   His foot shall tread th'oppressor down,
   His arms defend the righteous cause.

4. Let haughty sinners sink their pride,
   Nor lift so high their scornful head;
   But lay their foolish thoughts aside,
   And own the king that God hath made.

5. Such honors never come by chance,
   Nor do the winds promotion blow;
   Tis God the judge doth one advance,
   Tis God that lays another low,

6. No vain pretence to royal birth,
   Shall fix a tyrant on the throne;
   God, the great sovereign of the earth,
   Will rise and make his justice known.

7. His hand holds out the dreadful cup
   Of vengeance mixed with various plagues,
   To make the wicked drink them up,
   Wring out and taste the bitter dregs.

8. Now shall the Lord exalt the just;
   And while he tramples on the proud,
   And lays their glory in the dust,
   My lips shall sing his praise aloud.

B. Mycall "Power and government from God alone. Applied to the glorious revolution in America, July 4th, 1776."

1. To thee, most holy, and most high,
   To thee we bring our thankful praise;
   Thy works declare thy hand is nigh,
   Thy works of wonder and of grace.

2. America was doomed a slave,
   Her frame dissolved, her fears were great;
   When God a righteous council gave,
   To bear the pillars of the state.

3. They from thy power received their own,
   And swear to rule by wholesome laws;
   Thy foot shall tread oppressors down,
   Thy arm defend the righteous cause.

4. Let haughty sinners sink their pride,
   Nor lift so high their scornful head:
   But lay their foolish thoughts aside,
   And own the powers which God hath made.

5. As Watts

6. No vain pretence to royal birth
   Shall chain us to a tyrant's throne;
   God, the great Sovereign of the earth,
   Shall crush usurpers with his frown.

7. As Watts

8. Now shall the Lord exalt the just,
   And while he tramples on the proud,
   And lays their glory in the dust,
   Our lips shall sing his praise aloud.

C. Barlow LM: "Praise to God for the return of Peace"

1. To thee, most high and holy God,
   To thee our thankful hearts we raise;
   Thy works declare thy name abroad
   Thy wondrous works demand our praise.

2. To slavery doomed, thy chosen sons
   Beheld their foes triumphant rise;
   And sore oppressed by earthly thrones,
   They sought the sovereign of the skies.

3. Twas then, great God, with equal power,
   Arose thy vengeance and thy grace,
   To scourge their legions from the shore,
   And save the remnant of thy race.

4. Thy hand, that formed the restless main,
   And reared the mountain's awful head,
   Bade raging seas their course restrain,
   And desert wilds receive their dead.

5. Such wonders never come by chance,
   Nor can the winds such blessings blow;
   Tis God the judge doth one advance,
   Tis God that lays another low.

6. Let haughty tyrants sink their pride,
   Nor lift so high their scornful head;
   But lay their impious thoughts aside,
   And own the empire God hath made.

D. Dwight Proper meter: "Government from God alone. A Psalm for a General Election."

1. Thy praise, O Lord, our thankful songs renew;
   Thy present name thy works of wonder show,

Thy glorious works of wisdom, power and grace,
Thy sovereign blessings to our favored race;
The ruling God our peace and freedom prove,
And the glad tidings of forgiving love.

2. While from thy hand our rulers take their power
Give them thy greatness humbly to adore,
With hearts sincere to hold a righteous sway,
Bid justice triumph, and the proud obey,
Defend the poor, debasing bribes disdain,
Avenge bold wrongs, nor wield the sword in vain.

3. While round all realms wide dissolution's rolled
Give them the pillars of the earth t'uphold,
The meek, the wise, the faithful and the just,
And tread the vile oppressor in the dust;
To seek thy name, to love thy kingdom Lord,
And spread through earth the victories of thy word.

4. Give them the public weal alone to prize,
And each base purpose nobly to despise;
To bid pure knowledge round our borders shine,
And cheer the rising race with beams divine,
Examples bright of piety display,
And charm our sons to tread that lovely way.

5. Teach them, that greatness, power and place are thine,
Gifts from thy hand, bestowed for ends divine:
Rulers, thy Stewards, to mankind are given
To shower the good and build the cause of heaven;
From thee a rich reward the faithful know;
The faithless hasten to distinguished woe.

6. Thou art the Judge; thy scepter rules the skies;
At thy command the just to glory rise;
Thy fearful vengeance guilty wretches share,
Drink the last dregs, and plunge in deep despair;
To thy great name our raptured songs shall raise
A humble tribute of immortal praise.

11. Psalm 79 missing in Watts and Mycall

    A. Barlow LM: "For the distress of War."

        1. Behold, O God, what cruel foes,
Thy peaceful heritage invade;
Thy holy temple stands defiled,
In dust thy sacred walls are laid.

2. Wide o'er the valleys, drenched in blood,
   Thy people fall'n in death remain;
   The fowls of heaven their flesh devour,
   And savage beasts divide the slain.

3. Th'insulting foes, with impious rage,
   Reproach thy children to their face;
   "Where is your God of boasted power,
   "And where the promise of his grace."

4. Deep from the prison's horrid glooms,
   Oh hear the mournful captives sigh,
   And let thy sovereign power reprieve,
   The trembling souls condemned to die.

5. Let those, who dared insult thy reign,
   Return dismayed with endless shame,
   While heathens, who thy grace despise,
   Shall from thy vengeance learn thy name.

6. So shall thy children, freed from death,
   Eternal songs of honor raise,
   And every future age shall tell,
   Thy sovereign power and pardoning grace.

B. Dwight CM "Complaint of a Nation, or of the Church Against enemies."

1. O God attend, while hosts of foes
   Thy heritage invade;
   Thy Salem is become a heap;
   Thy house a ruin made.

2. Thy sons, denied a peaceful grave,
   Become the vultures food;
   Their bodies wolves insatiate tear,
   And lions drink their blood.

3. Behold us, Lord, a remnant sad,
   Of peace and hope forlorn,
   Of every mouth the vile reproach,
   Of every eye the scorn.

4. How long shall thy fierce anger burn?
   How long delay thy grace?
   How long thy hapless children mourn
   The hidings of thy face?

5. Thy vengeance shall find out our foes,
   Who mock thy fearful name,
   Who hate thy laws, deride thy word,
   And glory in their shame.

6. While they thy chosen flock devour,
And all our cities waste;
Forget our sins and follies past,
And let thy mercy haste.

7. Help, Lord of hosts, for Jesus' sake,
The glory of thy name;
Cleanse us from guilt, our hearts renew,
And wipe away our shame.

8. Why should our foes insulting cry,
"Where is the God you boast,
This fabled Lord of earth and heaven,
Your triumph and your trust?"

9. Arise, O God, and let thy hand
With awful glory shine;
With terror make our haughty foes
Confess thy name divine.

10. Behold our blood; our sighs regard,
And with almighty power
Rescue thy saints, condemned to die,
And bid us fear no more.

11. On them their soul reproach shall turn,
And wound with sevenfold scorn;
While we, thy flock, thy grace proclaim
To ages, yet unborn.

12. Psalm 88 missing in Watts and Mycall

A. Barlow as the 113th: "Loss of Friends, and absence of
Divine Grace."

1. O God of my salvation, hear
My nightly groan, my daily prayer,
That still employ my wasting breath;
My soul, declining to the grave,
Implores thy sovereign power to save
From dark despair and lasting death.

2. Thy wrath lies heavy on my soul,
And waves of sorrows o'er me roll,
While dust and silence spread the gloom:
My friends, belov'd in happier days,
The dear companions of my ways,
Descend around me to the tomb.

3. As, lost in lonely grief, I tread
   The mournful mansions of the dead,
   Or to some thronged assembly go;
   Through all alike I rove alone,
   While, here forgot and there unknown,
   The change renews my piercing woe.

4. And why will God neglect my call?
   Or who shall profit by my fall,
   When life departs and love expires?
   Can dust and darkness praise the Lord?
   Or wake, or brighten at his word,
   And tune the harp with heavenly quires?

5. Yet through each melancholy day,
   I've prayed to thee, and still will pray,
   Imploring still thy kind return—
   But oh! my friends, my comforts fled,
   And all my kindred of the dead
   Recall my wandering thoughts to mourn.

B. Dwight First Part CM "The Sorrows of Christ"

1. O God of my salvation, hear!
   My daily cry attend!
   When shall I triumph o'er the grave?
   And when my sorrows end?

2. My life is numbered with the dead,
   That lost in silence lie,
   My strength decays; my spirits droop,
   And all my comforts die.

3. Forgotten in the lowest pit,
   In darkness and the deep,
   My heart, the light of hope forsakes,
   My weary eyelids, sleep.

4. Shunned as polluted victims are,
   Like lepers, shut from men,
   My dearest friends my footsteps fly,
   Nor know my face again.

5. Each day a mourner from my youth,
   My tears in anguish fall;
   No feeling heart, partakes my pain;
   No ear attends my call.

6. Thy wrath hangs heavy o'er my head;
   Thy terrors round me burn;
   My feet are lost in sorrow's waves,
   Nor find a path to turn.

7. To thee each morn I raise my cry;
   Thy suppliant hear and save!
   Oh let me see thy smiling face,
   And bring me from the grave!

8. Though friend and lover, near and dear,
   In dark recesses hide;
   Though here I meet the darts of hate,
   And bear the scoffs of pride;

9. I'll lift my hands, I'll raise my eyes,
   For thy salvation, Lord;
   Thy hand shall save me from my foes,
   And well fulfill thy word.*

*Vitringa, Bishop Horne,etc. interpret this Psalm according to the scheme of the version here given.

C. Dwight Second Part LM: "Death not the end of our being. See Bishop Horne on these verses."

1. Shall man, O God of light, and life,
   Forever molder in the grave?
   Canst thou forget thy glorious work,
   Thy promise, and thy power to save?

2. In death's obscure, oblivious realms
   No truths are taught, nor wonders shown;
   No mercy beams to warn the heart;
   Thy name unsung, thy grace unknown.

3. No lips proclaim redeeming love,
   With praise and transport in the sound;
   The gospel's glory never shines,
   And hope and peace are never found.

4. But in those silent realms of night
   Shall peace and hope no more arise?
   No future morning light the tomb,
   Nor daystar gild the darksome skies?

5. Shall spring the faded world revive?
   Shall waning moons their light return?
   Again shall setting suns ascend,
   And the lost day anew be born?

6. Shall life revisit dying worms,
   And spread the joyful insect's wing?
   And oh shall man awake no more,
   To see thy face, thy name to sing?

7. Cease, cease, ye vain desponding fears;
   When Christ, our Lord, from darkness sprang,
   Death, the last foe, was captive led,
   And heaven with praise and wonder rang.

8. Him, the first fruits, his chosen sons
   Shall follow from the vanquished grave;
   He mounts his throne, the King of kings,
   His church to quicken, and to save.

9. Faith sees the bright, eternal doors
   Unfold, to make his children way;
   They shall be clothed with endless life,
   And shine in everlasting day.

10. The trump shall sound; the dust awake;
    From the cold tomb the slumberers spring;
    Through heaven with joy their myriads rise,
    And hail their Saviour and their King.

D. Dwight Third Part LM: "Life the only accepted time."

1. While life prolongs its precious light,
   Mercy is found, and peace is given;
   But soon, ah soon! approaching night
   Shall blot out every hope of heaven.

2. While God invites, how blessed the day!
   How sweet the gospel's charming sound!
   "Come sinners, haste, oh haste away,
   While yet a pardoning God he's found."

3. "Soon borne on time's most rapid wing,
   Shall death command you to the grave,
   Before his bar your spirits bring,
   And none be found to hear or save."

4. "In that lone land of deep despair,
   No Sabbath's heavenly light shall rise;
   No God regard your bitter prayer,
   Nor Saviour call you to the skies."

5. No wonders to the dead are shown,
   (The wonders of redeeming love;)
   No voice his glorious truth makes known,
   Nor sings the bliss of climes above.

6. Silence, and solitude, and gloom,
   In these forgetful realms appear,
   Deep sorrows fill the dismal tomb,
   And hope shall never enter there.

E. Dwight Fourth Part SM: "Solemn thoughts, after dangerous sickness."

1. Stretched on the bed of grief,
   In silence long I lay;
   For sore disease and wasting pain
   Had worn my strength away.

2. Just o'er the grave I hung;
   No pardon met my eyes;
   As blessings never greet the slain,
   And hope shall never rise.

3. Sweet mercy to my soul
   Revealed no charming ray;
   Before me rose a long, dark night,
   With no succeeding day.

4. I saw, beyond the tomb,
   That awful Judge appear,
   Prepared to scan with strict account
   My blessings wasted here.

5. His wrath, like flaming fire,
   Burned to the lowest hell,
   And in that hopeless world of woe
   He bade my spirit dwell.

6. My friends, now friends no more,
   At infinite remove,
   Left me, to gain their rich reward,
   And taste forgiving love.

7. Then O how vain appeared
   The joys beneath the sky!
   Like visions past, like flowers that blow,
   When wintry storms are nigh.

8. How mourned my sinking soul
   The Sabbath's hours divine
   The day of grace, that precious day,
   Consumed in sense and sin.

9. The work, the mighty work,
   Of life, so long delayed;
   Repentance, yet to be begun,
   Upon a dying bed!

10. Then to the Lord I prayed,
    And raised a bitter cry–
    "Hear me, O God, and save my soul,
    Lest I forever die."

11. He heard my humble cry;
    He saved my soul from death;
    To him I'll give my heart and hands,
    And consecrate my breath.

12. Ye sinners, fear the Lord,
    While yet tis called to day;
    Soon will the awful voice of death
    Command your souls away.

13. Soon will the harvest close;
    The summer soon be o'er;
    And soon your injured angry God
    Will hear your prayers no more.

13. Psalm 108 missing in Watts and Mycall

   A. Barlow CM: "A Song of Praise."

   1. Awake, my soul, to sound his praise,
      Awake my harp to sing;
      Join all my powers to song to raise,
      And morning incense bring.

   2. Among the people of his care,
      And through the nations round;
      Glad songs of praise will I prepare,
      And there his name resound.

   3. Be thou exalted, O my God,
      Above the starry train;
      Diffuse thy heavenly grace abroad,
      And teach the world thy reign.

   4. So shall thy chosen sons rejoice,
      And throng thy courts above;
      While sinners hear thy pardoning voice,
      And taste redeeming love.

   B. Dwight LM: "Praise to God for his care of the Church."

   1. Again, my tongue, thy silence break,
      My heart, and all my powers awake;
      My tongue, the glory of my frame,
      Awake, and sing Jehovah's name.

   2. Ye Saints rejoice; ye nations hear;
      While I your Maker's praise declare;
      High o'er the clouds his truth ascends;
      Through earth, through heaven his grace extends.

3. O'er heaven exalted is his throne;
   In every world his glory shown;
   Thy church, he loves, his hand shall save
   From death, and sorrow, and the grave.

4. Ye kingdoms, hear his awful voice!
   "In Zion shall my heart rejoice;
   This hand shall all her foes dismay,
   And make their scattered strength a prey."

5. "Mine are the sons of Zion, mine
   Their glory, grace, and truth divine;
   My scepter shines in Judah's hands,
   And still my strength in Ephraim stands."

6. "My foes to ruin shall be given,
   The shame of earth, the scorn of heaven;
   Their eyes shall see my church prevail;
   Their strength shall shrink, their courage fail."

7. O thou, beneath whose sovereign sway
   Nations, and worlds, in dust decay,
   Though thy sweet smile has been withdrawn,
   Thy aid denied, thy presence gone;

8. Yet wilt thou still with love return;
   With duty teach our hearts to burn;
   Our dying graces, Lord, revive,
   And bid thy fainting children live.

9. Save us from sin, and fear, and woe,
   From every snare and every foe,
   And help us boldly to contend,
   Falsehood resist, and truth defend.

14. Psalm 137 missing in Watts and Mycall

   A. Barlow "The Babylonian Captivity"

      1. Along the banks where Babel's current flows,
         Our captive bands in deep despondence strayed,
         While Zion's fall in sad remembrance rose,
         Her friends, her children mingled with the dead.

      2. The tuneless harp, that once with joy we strung,
         When praise employed and mirth inspired the lay,
         In mournful silence on the willows hung;
         And growing grief prolonged the tedious day.

      3. The barbarous tyrants, to increase the woe,
         With taunting smiles a song of Zion claim;

Bid sacred praise in strains melodious flow,
While they blaspheme the great Jehovah's name.

4. But how, in heathen chains and lands unknown,
Shall Israel's sons, a song of Zion raise?
O hapless Salem, God's terrestrial throne,
Thou land of glory, sacred mount of praise,

5. If e'er my memory lose thy lovely name,
If my cold heart neglect my kindred race,
Let dire destruction seize this guilty frame;
My hand shall perish and my voice shall cease.

6. Yet shall the Lord, who hears when Zion calls,
O'ertake her foes with terror and dismay,
His arm avenge her desolated walls,
And raise her children to eternal day.

B. Dwight LM First Part: "The sorrows of Israel in the Babylonian captivity."

1. By Babel's streams the Captives sat,
And wept for Zion's hapless fate;
Useless their harps on willows hung
While foes required a sacred song.

2. With taunting voice, and scornful eye,
"Sing us a song of heaven," they cry.
"While foes deride our God and King,
"How can we tune our harps to sing?"

3. "If Zion's woes our hearts forget,
"Or cease to mourn for Israel's fate,
"Let useful skill our hands forsake;
"Our hearts with hopeless sorrow break."

4. "Thou, ruined Salem, to our eyes
"Each day in sad remembrance rise!
"Should we e'er cease to feel thy wrongs,
"Lost be our joys, and mute our tongues."

5. "Remember Lord, proud Edom's sons,
"Who cried, exulting at our groans,
"While Salem trembled to her base,
"Raze them; her deep foundations raze."

6. While thus they sung, the mourners viewed
Their foes by Cyrus' arm subdued,
And saw his glory rise, who spread,
Their streets, and fields, with hosts of dead.

7. Pleased, they foresaw the blest decree,
   That set their tribes from bondage free,
   Renewed the temple, and restored
   The sacred worship of the Lord.

C. Dwight LM Second Part: "The Church's Complaint."

1. Lord, in these dark and dismal days,
   We mourn the hidings of thy face;
   Proud enemies our path surround,
   To level Zion with the ground.

2. Her songs, her worship, they deride,
   And hiss thy word with tongues of pride,
   And cry, t'insult our humble prayer,
   "Where is your God, ye Christians, where?"

3. Errors and sins and follies grow;
   Thy saints bow down in deepest woe;
   Their love decays, their zeal is o'er,
   And thousands walk with Christ no more.

4. To happier days our bosoms turn;
   Those days but teach us how to mourn;
   The God, who bade his mercy flow,
   In wrath withdraws his blessing now.

5. The blessing from thy truth's withdrawn;
   It's quickening, saving influence gone:
   Unwarned, unwakened, sinners hear,
   Nor see their awful danger near.

6. In dews unseen, or scanty showers,
   Thy spirit shed his healing powers;
   The thirsty ground is parched beneath,
   And all is barrenness and death.

7. Yet still thy name be ever blest,
   On thee our hope shall safely rest;
   Zion her Cyrus soon shall see
   Arrayed to set his Israel free.

8. Jesus, with vengeance armed shall come
   To crush his foes, and seal their doom,
   The mystic Babel whelm in dust,
   Her pomp, her idols, power and trust.

9. Then shall thy saints exult, and sing
   The matchless glories of their King;
   Nations before his altar bend,
   And peace from realm to realm extend.

D. Dwight SM Third Part: "Love to the Church."

1. I love thy kingdom, Lord,
    The house of thine abode,
    The church our blest Redeemer saved
    With his own precious blood.

2. I love thy Church, O God!
    Her walls before thee stand,
    Dear as the apple of thine eye,
    And graven on thy hand.

3. If e'er to bless thy sons
    My voice, or hands, deny,
    These hands let useful skill forsake,
    This voice in silence die.

4. If e'er my heart forget
    Her welfare, or her woe,
    Let every joy this heart forsake,
    And every grief o'erflow.

5. For her my tears shall fall;
    For her my prayers ascend;
    To her my cares and toils be given,
    Till toils and cares shall end.

6. Beyond my highest joy
    I prize her heavenly ways,
    Her sweet communion, solemn vows,
    Her hymns of love and praise.

7. Jesus, thou Friend divine,
    Our Saviour and our King,
    Thy hand from every snare and foe
    Shall great deliverance bring.

8. Sure as thy truth shall last,
    To Zion shall be given
    The brightest glories, earth can yield,
    And brighter bliss of heaven.

Bibliography

Primary Sources

Watts, Isaac. *The Psalms of David Imitated in the Language of the New Testament.* London: J. Clark, 1719.

Watts, Isaac. *The Psalms of David Imitated in the Language of the New Testament and applied to the Christian State and Worship.* Hartford: Patten and Webster, 1780.

Mycall, John. *The Psalms of David Imitated and applied to the Christian State and Worship.* Newburyport: John Mycall, 1781.

Barlow, Joel. *Doctor Watts Imitation of the Psalms of David, corrected and enlarged by Joel Barlow to which is added a collection of hymns, The whole applied to the state of the Christian Church in General.* Hartford: Barlow and Babcock, 1785.

Dwight, Timothy. *The Psalms of David Imitated in the Language of the New Testament and Applied to the Christian Use and Worship By I Watts, DD, A new edition in which the Psalms omitted by Dr. Watts are versified in proper meter by Timothy Dwight, DD.* Hartford: Hudson and Goodwin, 1801.

Secondary Sources

1. Methodology

Hoffman, Lawrence. *Beyond the Text: A Holistic Approach to Liturgy.* Bloomington: Indiana University Press, 1987.

Jay, Nancy. *Throughout Your Generations Forever.* Chicago: University of Chicago Press, 1992.

Kavanagh, Aidan. *On Liturgical Theology.* New York: Pueblo, 1984.

Ramshaw, Gail. *Christ in Sacred Speech.* Philadelphia: Fortress, 1986.

Taft, Robert. *Beyond East and West: Problems in Liturgical Understanding*. Washington D.C.: Pastoral Press, 1984.

Wilder, Amos. "Story and Story World" *Interpretation*. 37 (1983): 353–64.

———. *Theopoetic*. Philadelphia: Fortress, 1976.

Woltersdorff, Nicholas. "The Remembrance of Things (Not) Past: Philosophical Reflections on Christian Liturgy." In *Christian Philosophy*, edited by Thomas P. Flint. Notre Dame: University of Notre Dame Press, 1990.

Wren, Brian. *What Language Shall I Borrow?*. New York: Crossroad, 1989.

2. Church Music and Psalmody

Bailey, Albert Edward. *The Gospel in Hymns*. New York: Charles Scribner's Sons, 1950.

Baker, Frank. "The Sources of John Wesley's 'Collection of Psalms and Hymns' Charleston, 1737." *John Wesley's First Hymn-Book*. Frank Baker and George Williams, eds. London: Wesley Historical Society, 1964, xxvii–xxviv.

Benson, Louis F. "The American Revisions of Watts's 'Psalms'."- *Journal of the Presbyterian Historical Society*. 2 (1903–04): 18–34, 75–89.

———. *The English Hymn*. Philadelphia: Presbyterian Board of Publication, 1915.

Bishop, Selma L. *Isaac Watts Hymns and Spiritual Songs (1707)*. Ann Arbor: The Pierian Press, 1974.

Brueggemann, Walter. *Israel's Praise*. Philadelphia: Fortress, 1988.

Crawford, Richard. *The Core Repertory of Early American Psalmody*. Madison: A-R Editions, 1984.

Creamer, David. *Methodist Hymnology*. New York: Joseph Longking, 1848.

Daggett, O. E. "The Psalms in Worship." *The New Englander*. July, 1846: 312–31.

Foote, Henry Wilder. *Three Centuries of American Hymnody*. Cambridge, Massachusetts: Harvard University Press, 1940.

Glass, Alexander Henry. *The Story of the Psalters*. London: Kegan Paul, Trench and Co., 1888.

Gould, Nathaniel. *Church Music in America*. Boston: A. N. Johnson, 1853.

Haraszti, Zoltan. *The Enigma of the Bay Psalm Book*. Chicago: University of Chicago Press, 1956.

Leaver, Robin A. "English Metrical Psalmody." in *The Hymnal 1982 Companion*, edited by Raymond F. Glover, 321–48. New York: Church Hymnal Corporation, 1990.

————. 'Goostly Psalmes and Spirituall Songs': English and Dutch Metrical Psalms from Coverdale to Utenhove 1535–1566. Oxford: Clarendon Press, 1991.

————."Isaac Watts' Hermeneutical Principles and the Decline of English Metrical Psalmody." in *Churchman* 92 (1978): 56–60.

MacDougall, Hamilton C. *Early New England Psalmody*. Brattleboro: Stephen Daye Press, 1940.

Manns, Charles. "Psalmody in America to the Civil War." In *The Hymnal 1982 Companion*, edited by Raymond F. Glover, 393–416. New York: Church Hymnal Corporation, 1990.

Marini, Stephen. "Rehearsal for Revival: Sacred Singing and the Great Awakening." In *Sacred Sound: Music in Religious Thought and Practice*, edited by Joyce Irwin, 71–91. Chico, California: Scholar's Press, 1983.

Ninde, Edward S. *The Story of the American Hymn*. New York: Abingdon, 1921.

Phelps, Austin et al. *Hymns and Choirs*. Andover: Warren Draper, 1860.

Winship, George Parker. *The Cambridge Press 1638–1692: A Reexamination of the Evidence Concerning the Bay Psalm Book and the Eliot Indian Bible*. Philadelphia: University of Pennsylvania Press, 1945.

Worst, William. *New England Psalmody 1760–1810 Analysis of an American Idiom*. Ph.D. diss., University of Michigan, 1974.

Young, Carlton. "John Wesley's 1737 Charlestown *Collection of Psalms and Hymns*." *The Hymn* 41 (October 1990): 19–27.

3. Psalters and Tunebooks

Allen, F. D. *The New York Selection of Sacred Music*. New York: Bartlett and Raynor, 1833.

The Chorister's Companion. New Haven: Simeon Jocelin, 1788.

Christian Psalmody in four parts; comprising Dr. Watts's Psalms abridged; Dr. Watts's Hymns abridged; select hymns from other authors; and select Harmony. Boston: Samuel Armstrong, 1815.

The Church Psalmist. Philadelphia: Presbyterian Publication Committee, 1847.

A Facsimile Reprint of the First Edition of the Bay Psalm Book. New York: Burt Franklin, 1973.

The Federal Harmony. Boston: John Norman, 1792.

Hastings, Thomas and William Patton. *The Christian Psalmist*. New York: Ezra Collier, 1836.

Holyoke, Samuel. *The Christian Harmonist*. Salem, Massachusetts: Joshua Cushing, 1804.

Mason, Lowell and David Greene. *Church Psalmody: A Collection of Psalms and Hymns adapted to Public Worship*. Boston: Perkins and Marvin, 1831.

Pilsbury, Amos. *The United States Sacred Harmony*. Boston: Isaiah Thomas and Ebenezer Andrews, 1799.

Psalms and Hymns adapted to the Public Worship of the Presbyterian Church. Philadelphia: J. Whetham, 1835.

Psalms and Hymns for Christian Use and Worship. New Haven: Durrie and Peck, 1845. (This is the General Association of Connecticut's Psalter).

The Psalms and Hymns of Dr. Watts, Arranged by Dr. Rippon; with Dr. Rippon's Selection. Philadelphia: David Clark, 1839.

The Psalms and Hymns of the Reformed Protestant Dutch Church in North America. Philadelphia: Mentz and Rovoudt, 1847.

Sternhold, T. and Hopkins, I. *The Whole Book of Psalms collected into English Meeter*. London: Company of Stationers, 1618.

The Village Harmony or Youth's Assistant to Sacred Music. Exeter, New Hampshire: Norris and Sawyer, 1803 and 1807.

Watts, Isaac. *Hymns and Spiritual Songs with an Essay Towards the Improvement of Christian Psalmody by the Use of Evangelical Hymns in Worship as well as the Psalms of David*. London: J. Humphries, 1707.

Webb, George James. *The Massachusetts Collection of Psalmody*. Boston: Crocker and Brewster, 1840.

Wesley, John. *Collection of Psalms and Hymns*. Charlestown: Lewis Timothy, 1737. Facsimile reprint by Nashville: United Methodist Publishing House, 1988.

Winchell, James M. *Arrangement of the Psalms Hymns and Spiritual Songs of the Rev. Isaac Watts DD*. Boston: James Loring, 1818.

Worcester, Samuel. *The Psalms, Hymns and Spiritual Songs of the Rev. Isaac Watts, D.D. to which are added Select Hymns from other authors*. Boston: Samuel Armstrong, 1823.

4. The Context: History, Theology, Biography

Anonymous. "Joel Barlow." *The New Englander*. 124 (July, 1873): 413–30.

Atkins, Gaius and Frederick Fagley. *History of American Congregationalism*. Boston: The Pilgrim Press, 1942.

Baldwin, Alice. *The New England Clergy and the American Revolution*. Durham: Duke University Press, 1928.

Bassett, Joseph. "The New England Way and Vatican II." *The Unitarian Universalist Christian*. 361 (1981): 59.

Bentley, William. *The Diary of William Bentley*. Gloucester, Massachusetts: Peter Smith, 1962.

Berk, Stephen E. *Calvinism versus Democracy: Timothy Dwight and the Origins of American Evangelical Orthodoxy*. Hamden, Conn: Archon Books, 1974.

Birdsall, "The Second Great Awakening and the New England Social Order." *Church History*. 39 (1970): 345-64.

Bonomi, Patricia U. *Under the Cope of Heaven*. New York: Oxford University Press, 1986.

Buckingham, Joseph T. *Specimens of Newspaper Literature*. 1850; reprint, Vol. I. Freeport, NY: Books for Libraries Press, 1971.

Carroll, Peter N. *Religion and the Coming of the American Revolution*. Waltham, Massachusetts: Ginn-Blaisdell, 1970.

Cowie, Alexander. *John Trumbull Connecticut Wit*. Chapel Hill: University of North Carolina Press, 1936.

Cuningham, Charles. *Timothy Dwight 1752–1817*. New York: Macmillan, 1942.

Davies, Horton. *The Worship of the American Puritans, 1629-1730*. New York: Peter Lang, 1990.

Dwight, Timothy. *The Nature and Danger of Infidel Philosophy*. New Haven, 1798.

———. *The Major Poems of Timothy Dwight*. William McTaggart and William Bottorff, eds. Gainesville, Florida: Scholars' Facsimiles and Reprints, 1969.

———. "Observations on Language." *Memoirs of the Connecticut Academy of Arts and Sciences*. Vol I. New Haven: Oliver Steele, 1806.

Escott, Harry. *Isaac Watts Hymnographer*. London: Independent Press, 1962.

Fountain, David. *Isaac Watts Remembered*. Worthing: Henry Walter, 1974.

Griswold, Rufus W. *The Poets and Poetry of America*. Philadelphia: Carey and Hart, 1843.

Hall, David. *Worlds of Wonder, Days of Judgement*. New York: Alfred Knopf, 1989.

Handy, Robert T. *A Christian America*. Second Edition. New York: Oxford University Press, 1984.

Hatch, Nathan O. *The Democratization of American Christianity*. New Haven: Yale University Press, 1989.

Hatfield, Edwin F. *The Poets of the Church*. Boston: Milford House, 1884.

Hathaway, Richard. *Sylvester Judd's New England*. University Park: Pennsylvania State University Press, 1981.

Howard, Leon. *The Connecticut Wits*. Chicago: University of Chicago Press, 1943.

Kafer, Peter. "The Making of Timothy Dwight." *William and Mary Quarterly*. 47 (April 1990): 189–209.

Keller, Charles. *The Second Great Awakening in Connecticut*. New Haven: Yale University Press, 1942.

Koch, G. Adolf. *Religion and the American Enlightenment*. New York: Thomas Crowell, 1968.

Kucklick, Bruce. *Churchmen and Philosophers*. New Haven: Yale University Press, 1985.

May, Henry F. *The Enlightenment in America*. New York: Oxford University Press, 1976.

Mead, Sidney. *The Lively Experiment: The Shaping of Christianity in America*. New York: Harper and Row, 1963.

Morgan, Edmund S. "The Puritan Ethic and the American Revolution." In *Puritanism and the American Experience*, edited by Michael McGiffert. Reading, Mass: Addison-Wesley, 1969.

Noll, Mark A. *A History of Christianity in the United States and Canada*. Grand Rapids: Eerdmans, 1992.

Nugent, Walter. *Structures of American Social History*. Bloomington: Indiana University Press, 1981.

Parrington, Vernon Louis. *The Connecticut Wits*. Hamden, Connecticut: Archon Books, 1963.

Proceedings of the Massachusetts Historical Society. IX, X. Boston: The Society, 1896.

Purcell, Richard. *Connecticut in Transition 1775–1818*. Washington D.C.: American Historical Society, 1918.

Shiels, Richard. "The Second Great Awakening in Connecticut: Critique of the Traditional Interpretation." *Church History*. 49 (1980): 401–15.

Silverman, Kenneth. *Timothy Dwight*. New York: Twayne, 1969.

Stackhouse, Rochelle. "Hymns of Love and Praise: A Brief History of Music in American Congregational Churches." *Prism* 8 (Spring 1993): 38–52.

Steiner, Walter, M.D. "Dr. Lemuel Hopkins, One of the Celebrated Hartford Wits, and a Forgotten, Distinguished American Student of Tuberculosis." *Johns Hopkins Hospital Bulletin* 21 (January 1910): 16–27.

Dexter, Franklin, ed. *The Literary Diary of Ezra Stiles*. New York: Scribner's, 1901.

Thacher, James M. *American Medical Biography*. Boston: 1828.

Thomas, Isaiah. *The History of Printing in America*. Boston, 1810; reprint, Barre, Massachusetts: Imprint Society, 1970.

Todd, Charles Burr. *Life and Letters of Joel Barlow, LLD*. New York: Putnam's, 1886.

Trumbull, John. "Lines Addressed to Messrs. Dwight and Barlow."

In *The Poetical Works of John Trumbull*. Hartford: Samuel G. Goodrich, 1820.

Tyler, Moses. *Three Men of Letters*. New York: G.P. Putnam's Sons, 1895.

Walker, Williston. *A History of the Congregational Churches in the United States*. New York: Christian Literature Company, 1894.

Wenzke, Anabelle S. *Timothy Dwight (1752–1817)*. Lewiston, New York: Edwin Mellen Press, 1989.

White, James F. *Protestant Worship: Traditions in Transition*. Louisville: Westminster/John Knox, 1989.

Woodress, James. *A Yankee's Odyssey: The Life of Joel Barlow*. Philadelphia: J.P. Lippincott, 1958.

Zunder, Theodore. *The Early Days of Joel Barlow*. New Haven: Yale University Press, 1934.

5. Local Church and Denominational Histories

Carr, Mrs. William et al. *History, Annals and Sketches of the Central Church of Fall River, Massachusetts*. Boston: Fort Hill Press, 1905.

Caulkins, Frances Manwaring. *History of New London, Connecticut*. New London: published by the author, 1852.

Chandler, Edward Herrick. *The History of the Wellesley Congregational Church*. Boston: Benjamin H. Sanborn, 1898.

Chandler, Seth. *History of the Town of Shirley Massachusetts*. Shirley: Published by the Author, 1883.

The Commemorative Services of the First Church in Newton Massachusetts on the Occasion of the Two Hundred and Twenty-fifth Anniversary of its Foundation. Boston: Rockwell and Churchill, 1890.

Eversull, Henry Kelso. *The Evolution of an Old New England Church*. East Haven: Tuttle, Morehouse and Taylor, 1924.

Gilman, Samuel. *Memoirs of a New England Village Choir with Occasional Reflections*. Boston: S.G. Goodrich, 1829.

Hanson, Muriel R. *A History of the First Congregational Church of Ridgefield 1712–1962*. Ridgefield: First Congregational Church, 1962.

Historical Manual of the South Church in Andover, Massachusetts. Andover: Warren Draper, 1859.

Hoyt, James S. *The First Evangelical Congregational Church*. Cambridge, Massachusetts: Harvard University Press, 1878.

Jennings, Isaac. *The One Hundred Year Old Meetinghouse of the Church of Christ in Bennington, Vermont*. Cambridge, Massachusetts: Riverside Press, 1907.

McKenzie, Alexander. *Lectures on the History of the First Church in Cambridge*. Boston: Congregational Publishing Society, 1873.

Neale, R.H. *Address at Two Hundredth Anniverary of First Baptist Church*. Boston: privately printed, 1865.

Noyes, Harriette Eliza. *A Memorial History of Hampstead New Hampshire Congregational Church, 1752–1902*. Volume II. Boston: George Reed, 1903.

Parker, Edwin Pond. *History of the Second Church of Christ in Hartford*. Hartford: Belknap and Warfield, 1892.

Potter, James H. *Church of Christ (Congregational) Norfolk, Connecticut, Two Hundred Years*. Norfolk: [n.p.], 1960.

The Records of the General Association of the Colony of Connecticut, June 20, 1738–June 19, 1799. Hartford: Case, Lockwood and Brainard, 1888.

Shuster, Ruth. *Gathered in 1707*. Braintree, Massachusetts: First Congregational Church, 1957.

Walker, George Leon. *History of the First Church in Hartford 1633–1883*. Hartford: Brown and Gross, 1884.

Index

Above Bar Independent Church (Southampton, Eng.), 35

aesthetic changes of language in Psalters, 40, 71, 93. *See also* language and change; *See also* liturgical language

𝕽"Along the banks where Babel's current flows" (Psalm 137, Barlow). *See* Psalm 137 B

American revisions of Watts' Psalters, impact of, 110

American Revolution, 15–27; in Connecticut, 17, 19, 23

Andover, Mass. Second Church. *See* Church (Andover, Mass.)

Arminianism, 12, 13

Babcock, Elisha, 48, 61

Baldwin, Ruth. *See* Barlow, Ruth Baldwin

Barlow, Joel (1754–1812), 3, 130; admitted to Connecticut bar, 56; association with Thomas Jefferson, 57; co-publisher of *The American Mercury*, 48; early life, 46; hermeneutic, 116, 120; influence of his Psalter revision on Dwight's Psalter revision, 87–96; later life, 57; ministry as chaplain, 47–48; philosophy of, 49,

56–57; portrait removed from Yale College, 59; Presbyterian usage of his Psalter revision, 110–11; reception of his Pslater revision, 53–54, 55; reputation, 58, 108, 114; service in Washington's army, 47; travels, 57, 58; works: *Doctor Watts Imitation of the Psalms of David. See also* Psalters. *Doctor Watts Imitation of the Psalms of David;—The Vision of Columbus,* 48, 57; at Yale College, 47

Barlow, Ruth Baldwin, 47, 57, 59

Barnard, John, 43

Bay Psalm Book. *See* Psalters, *The Whole Book of Psalms Faithfully Translated into English Metre*

Benson, Louis, xi, 5, 14n25, 39n34, 44n2, 44n3, 45n8, 56, 58, 68n99, 100, 105,107n40, 110

Bentley, William, 100

biblical language, fidelity to, 116

Billings, William, 14, 84; *The New-England Psalm-Singer,* 101

Boston, Mass. First Baptist Church. *See* First Baptist Church (Boston, Mass.)

Braintree, Mass. First Congregational Church. *See* First Congre-

189

About the Author

The **Rev. Dr. Rochelle Stackhouse** received her Ph.D. in Liturgical Studies in 1994 from Drew University in Madison, New Jersey. She was ordained in the United Church of Christ in 1982, and she has served churches in Michigan and New York. She taught worship and preaching as an adjunct at both Lancaster and New Brunswick seminaries. Currently she serves as senior pastor of the United Church of Christ of Norwell, Massachusetts and teaches on the adjunct faculty of Hartford Seminary. She is married to P. Gavin Ferriby, an academic librarian currently pursuing a Ph.D. in Medieval Church History. They are parents to three-year-old Luke and have just adopted their daughter Leah who, like their son, has come from South Korea.

GENERAL THEOLOGICAL SEMINARY
NEW YORK